WHAT PEOPLE ARE SAYING ABOUT DR. BURGDORF ...

I have known Dr. Mike Burgdorf since we played football together at the University of Notre Dame. Together we have moved through the many challenges of life with similar fervor in our professional, personal, and social lives. It has been great to have him by my side through the years for discussions and advice on how to keep our edge as age has matured us, but not slowed us down. As an ER doctor, I have to gain the confidence and trust of my patients in a short period of time. Feeling and looking your best is critical at all times. Dr. Burgdorf can help anyone conquer the exterior challenges brought on by aging.

Mark Monahan, MD

Trauma and emergency medicine specialist

I played twenty-four years of organized football and worked out for a living until retiring from the NFL after the 2005 season. I was fortunate enough to play for nine years and be a Super Bowl XXXVI Champion as a player for the Patriots. I knew it would be difficult to maintain myself without the structure I was accustomed to having ... someone telling me how to eat and how to train. I didn't want the "dad body" that would come from letting myself go. I've had to change the way I train, what I put into my body, and actually start working on my appearance for the first time in my life. For all you dads staring back at your own "dad bod" in the mirror, I encourage you to hit the gym, watch what you eat, and pick up a copy of *The Daddy Do Over* to get your confidence back. I've been out of the NFL for over ten years and I am still well under my playing weight.

Marc Edwards

Former Fighting Irish captain
Nine-year NFL player
Super Bowl XXXVI Champion

As a barbershop and salon owner, I get to see the impact to one's confidence when appearances are enhanced. It's simple; when you look good, you feel good. Dr. Burgdorf is a no-nonsense, authentic man's man who appreciates making people feel their best. In this book, Dr. Burgdorf tackles areas few men want to face but should. His aim is to help others regain confidence, allowing them to step into a room with their heads high. Need a confident booster? *The Daddy Do Over* could be your answer.

Matt Fine

Owner of The Blockhouse Barbershop and Lunatic Fringe Salon

Even as a Notre Dame student athlete, Dr. Mike Burgdorf has demonstrated unparalleled character and the utmost of integrity. I knew early on that he would be successful. In short, he is unbelievable.

Lou Holtz

2008 college football Hall of Fame
University of Notre Dame legendary coach

As a busy professional about to turn fifty, I want to look and feel my best and work hard to stay fit. Looking and feeling good is very important to me. I want to age gracefully, but also want to look my best. That's why I run, lift, and eat well. To me, having a conversation with a good plastic surgeon falls within the same vein. Why wouldn't I entertain the modern clinical options that are available to me? The ladies in our lives have been having makeovers for years; why shouldn't we men avail ourselves of the same technology? Why not explore a Daddy Do-Over?

Lawrence J. Skok, Esq.

Senior legal counsel
Federal Realty Investment Trust

THE

DADDY

DO OVER

THE

DADDY

DO OVER

BOOST YOUR CONFIDENCE IN THE
BOARDROOM AND THE BEDROOM

MICHAEL R. BURGDORF, MD, MPH

Published by Advantage, Charleston, South Carolina.
Member of Advantage Media Group.

ADVANTAGE is a registered trademark, and the Advantage colophon is a trademark of Advantage Media Group, Inc.

Printed in the United States of America.

10 9 8 7 6 5 4 3 2 1

ISBN: 978-1-64225-010-7
LCCN: 2018931978

Cover and layout design by George Stevens.

This publication is designed to p ovide accurate and authoritative information in regard to the subject matter covered. It is sold with the understanding that the publisher is not engaged in rendering legal, accounting, or other professional services. If legal advice or other expert assistance is required, the services of a competent professional person should be sought.

Advantage Media Group is proud to be a part of the Tree Neutral® program. Tree Neutral offsets the number of t ees consumed in the production and printing of this book by taking proactive steps such as planting trees in direct proportion to the number of trees used to print books. To learn more about Tree Neutral, please visit www.treeneutral.com.

Advantage Media Group is a publisher of business, self-improvement, and professional development books and online learning. We help entrepreneurs, business leaders, and professionals share their Stories, Passion, and Knowledge to help others Learn & Grow. Do you have a manuscript or book idea that you would like us to consider for publishing? Please visit advantagefamily.com or call 1.866.775.1696.

DEDICATION

As I sit to write this, my niece is waiting to be born via C-section. I remember the day I first became a father and the three additional times after that. I remember the emotion and high excitement I felt waiting to meet *my* child. It was pride, fear, excitement, love, and anticipation all wrapped together. Being a dad is the best thing, and the hardest thing, I've ever done. While this book focuses essentially on the outside of a dad, the insides of a dad are even more important. I am grateful for the process of being a dad and the ability—more frequently than I would like to admit—to have a Daddy Do-Over with my kids. Thanks, gang. I love each one of you more than you can comprehend.

TABLE OF CONTENTS

PART I
GETTING TO WORK

PART II
PREP WORK

PART III
PROCEDURES

WHAT IS THE DADDY DO-OVER?

t's hard for guys to admit that we need help in anything. It doesn't matter if it's finding the missing remote, repairing a crankshaft, or realizing that we could actually do something about those love handles if we'd only ask. We don't like to admit defeat, even if that defeat is handed down by Mother Nature herself.

I know. I'm a guy—a regular joe who enjoys a good beer, grew up in New Jersey, played linebacker for Notre Dame, and got into plastic surgery because I wanted to increase my patients' confidence and improve their lives and relationships. And recently, more of my patients have been dads.

I understand the stigma around male plastic surgery. Many guys think of it as "feminine," or as an admission that they need help in some area or another. But the thing is, we *do* need the help. We may get more of a break when it comes to aging—a touch of gray, a little thickness around the waist, and some crow's feet can be attractive in men—but there are some things we just can't power through. I've seen fear of this stigma lead to avoidance and denial of easily accessible help—help that would have prevented erosion of confidence, dissolution of marriage, loss of career.

That's why I wrote this book. I want guys to understand that there are options for looking younger, restoring your self-confidence, and making it all look natural. Those options, which I call the Daddy Do-Over, consist of a combination of procedures aimed at each guy's individual concerns and desires. The Daddy Do-Over involves surgical and/or nonsurgical interventions that'll have you feeling like a better version of yourself. You're not going to come out looking like one of those D-list celebrity disasters. Instead, the goal is to restore your self-confidence and give you back the look you want. You're going to come out with renewed confidence that will trickle over to your results in the boardroom … and, quite possibly, the bedroom.

This book is for dads of all types—businessmen, baby boomers, weekend warriors, dads-to-be (like grooms, single guys, etc.)—everyone from construction workers to white collar executives to musicians to professional athletes. There are all kinds of factors in a dad's life that he's either dealt with since birth or that are taking their toll on him through work stress, home stress, or just life in general. If you are this type of dad, this book is for you.

If you are the type of dad who has it all together, looks great and feels great—the so-called "Superdad" who handles things all on his own—this book may NOT be for you. Or it might be, if you want to keep those looks as you get older, improve your high confidence as you age, and continue excelling in every endeavor in life. This book is also NOT for you if you aren't willing to invest the time, energy, and resources into maintaining your appearance. (In this book, though, I'll actually show you how you can get a strong ROI with your own plastic surgery.) If you are too good for plastic surgery or think only women have "work done," you might consider putting this book down now—or you could read on to see that many men once thought like you and have been "corrected" by their wives or doctors and are now realizing the results of boosting their confidence in the boardroom and the bedroom with their own Daddy Do-Overs. Before you close the book, take a look at the next section, regarding some misunderstandings about male plastic surgery.

DADDY DO-OVER MYTHS

MYTH: Plastic surgery is only for women.

REALITY: Statistics disagree. As an example, in 2016 alone over 40 percent of all breast reductions were performed on MEN. As a percentage of total patients, the male population visiting a cosmetic plastic surgeon's practice has risen from 2–3 percent to upward of 12–15 percent.[1] This topic is covered further in chapter 2.

MYTH: I'm a successful businessman. I get paid based on results, not on my appearance.

REALITY: If you believe that, try showing up to the next board meeting in flip-flops and a Hawaiian shirt. Statistics show that attractive people actually make more money than unattractive ones.[2] Why wouldn't you give yourself every advantage possible? Your competition

1   "2016 Plastic Surgery Statistics Report," American Society of Plastic Surgeons, accessed December 4, 2017, https://www.plasticsurgery.org/documents/News/Statistics/2016/cosmetic-procedures-men-2016.pdf.

2   David DiSalvo, "Science Asks: Do Pretty People Really Make More Money?" *Forbes Magazine* website, February 21, 2017, https://www.forbes.com/sites/daviddisalvo/2017/02/21/science-asks-do-pretty-people-really-make-more-money/#670cf3c52dbd.

certainly does. This topic is covered further in chapter 2.

MYTH: If you have liposuction, you can't regain weight in that area.

REALITY: Yes, you can. With large weight gain, you can actually eat through the liposuction. This topic is covered further in chapter 15.

MYTH: I'm a guy—I don't have to worry about my appearance.

REALITY: This one is true. If you want to be alone for the rest of your life, with a minimum-wage job, and no hope for success in your future. This topic is covered further in chapter 2.

MYTH: Gynecomastia (man boobs) can be cured with regular exercise.

REALITY: You may be able to mask it by working out a bit, but you're not going to solve it. Sometimes genetics play a significant role. This topic is covered further in chapter 14.

MYTH: Plastic surgery isn't safe.

REALITY: All surgery has some risk, but plastic surgery is very safe when performed by an experienced, board-certified plastic surgeon. This topic is covered further in chapter 6.

MYTH: I will turn gay or into a metrosexual if I have plastic surgery.

REALITY: Being aware of your appearance doesn't change your sexual orientation or make you any less of a "man," just a better-looking one. This topic is covered further in chapter 4.

MYTH: You will look plastic or fake after the surgery.

REALITY: A skilled surgeon will give you natural-looking results. Subtlety is key. This topic is covered further in chapters 2 and 4.

MYTH: Wrinkles are "distinguishing" characteristics in men.

REALITY: Yes, a little aging is an attractive feature, but just like everything else in life, moderation is key. This topic is covered further in chapter 9.

MYTH: Plastic surgery will be noticeable, especially on my "rugged good looks."

REALITY: It's awfully hard to keep the "good looks" part if all one sees are those "rugged" wrinkles, that spare tire, and your man boobs. Again, subtlety is key to a natural appearance. No one is trying to turn you into a human Ken doll. This topic is covered further in chapter 2.

MYTH: I can't afford it.

REALITY: Yes, plastic surgery costs real money and is not covered by insurance. Think of it as an investment in yourself. How much will it cost if you get passed over for the promotion because you "don't look up to the task"? What is that ROI? This topic is covered further in chapter 2.

MYTH: Everybody will know I had surgery.

REALITY: Only if you tell them—which I hope you do, and that you refer them to me as patients. This topic is covered further in chapter 6.

MYTH: I can lift my way through these man boobs.

REALITY: While exercise can build up the chest muscles underneath the skin and breast tissue, oftentimes it will not eliminate the male pattern breast tissue. This topic is covered further in chapter 14.

MYTH: I can't afford the downtime from plastic surgery.

REALITY: Men tend to be more resistant to surgical downtime, but with the newer non-invasive technologies, more options exist with limited downtime. This topic is covered further in chapter 8.

MYTH: Plastic surgery will make me a new person, one who is irresistible and immune to rejection.

REALITY: Plastic surgery can change your appearance and help you demonstrate more confidence. It will NOT make you irresistible to every creature on earth, nor immune to rejection. We hope it will allow you to exude more confidence and impact your relationships positively. However, if your personality has fatal flaws (like believing women deserve physical abuse), no amount of plastic surgery will fix that. Go get some help. This topic is covered further in chapter 4.

MYTH: Men are supposed to look "old"—it's just expected.

REALITY: Yes, men do have it a bit easier than women in this department, but who wants to be mistaken as Grandpa when dropping your daughter off at college? This topic is covered further in chapter 2.

FROM NOTRE DAME LINEBACKER TO PLASTIC SURGEON DAD

D ads today are different, as is the family dynamic. Fathers tend to participate more deeply in the day-to-day lives of their children. They are involved with raising kids, spending increased time at home, and are just more present in their kids' lives. Most couples seem to have dual responsibility for the kids, as often both parents work outside the home. Dads understand the harried schedule that used to be reserved only for moms running the kids all over town. They are now involved with some of the extra sacrifices it takes to be a successful parent— and by "successful" I mean getting kids to activities relatively on time, with mostly all the equipment needed, having fed them far enough in advance so that they won't hurl during the activity. Dads are now more used to forgoing their gym time, eating like garbage with the kids at the drive-through, and neglecting their own sleep in order to take care of the baby. Dads now share in these responsibilities, and it is showing.

I know. I've seen the effects of raising kids with the passing years. I've noticed my own appearance deteriorate with the more children I have (I'm the proud dad of four great kids) and as the responsibilities of my practice grow. I'm certainly seeing the graying of more hair and an increase in wrinkles. It's a struggle that a lot of today's dads—and men in general—face and one that I can strongly relate to.

NO SKINNY JEANS
FOR THIS GUY

To give you perspective and some reassurance that I'm not some waif-type, vegan-eating, ultra-feminine guy, let me share some of my background with you. I consider myself a bit of a hybrid between a Man's Man and a compassionate Gentleman Surgeon. The type of man who enjoys college football, a good burger, and the occasional cigar, who is also at ease in a tuxedo, drinking a cabernet, and escorting my beautiful wife to a charity ball. The type of meticulous surgeon who pays strict attention to all the details, but who can still hold a normal, caring conversation with patients' families after the surgery. I sport a goatee, salt-and-pepper hair, stand six-foot-one, and weigh 210 pounds. I grew up in New Jersey and married a Southern belle. I get pissed off at my kids pretty frequently, love my family passionately, and try to continue to be romantic with my wife of more than sixteen years. I can speak appropriately with nice manners, and I can just as easily slip back to my locker room and Jersey days by using the finest expletives in the land. I believe in and rely upon God, strive to be a good person, and want to enjoy my life to the fullest extent. All in all, I try to remain true to who I am as a person and what I stand for while trying to make whomever I am speaking with comfortable in the given situation.

INTEGRITY IN CHANGING LIVES

During my football days at Notre Dame, my coach, Lou Holtz, stressed living a life of integrity. One of his favorite sayings was, "Do the right thing." He punctuated our Friday night practices with a relaxation session during which he would talk to us about being honest with ourselves. "Men, you can fool the television cameras, the fans, even your friends and family ... but not yourself. At the end of the day, you have to look at yourself in the mirror and know that what you did was the right thing to do." I hold this philosophy dear in my life. I want it to always be a part of my character, I teach it to my own children, and I founded my practice, Music City Plastic Surgery, on its foundation.

When it comes to plastic surgery, "doing the right thing" translates to using my skills to restore self-confidence in my patients, improving their lives and helping them see themselves in a renewed light. Plastic surgery allows me to have a significant impact on many peoples' lives. What's exciting for me is that the impact seems to extend like a ripple in the water. I help make changes, often secretively, on the outside of an individual. Then I can be a witness to the countless changes that occur on the inside of that same person. The affect on people within that person's sphere can be profound. With the Daddy Do-Over, that ripple effect can permeate through an entire family.

The specific procedures for a Daddy Do-Over are important, as are the skills of the individual surgeon. I am aware, however, that my ability to make these changes in someone else is not solely dependent on my skill or the procedures chosen. I depend on God for the skills I have and the opportunities I receive. Before each surgery, I ask him to guide me and my hands and allow me to achieve the results I am trying to obtain and which the patient desires.

With guys, I understand that it's tough to ask about these procedures. We don't like to admit that we need help from anyone. The hope with this book is that it gives you the opportunity to do some research into these options from the comfort of your own home, without having to go out and admit to some doctor you've never met before that you can't get rid of that double chin, or that last layer of fat over your six-pack, without help.

To make it easier for you to analyze your options, this book is divided into three parts:

Part I: Getting to Work talks about the growing trend of male plastic surgery, what procedures are topping the charts, and what types of men are getting what kinds of surgery and why—the answers may surprise you.

Part II: Prep Work is your game plan. If you're considering plastic surgery, this is the step-by-step on what to expect, how to prepare, and best practices for recovery.

Part III: Procedures lays out the surgical and nonsurgical interventions available. You can jump right to this part if you're just curious about what plastic surgery can do for anything from sweaty feet to man boobs. And if you have more questions, my contact information is at the back of the book.

All warmed up? Let's get to it. Ready ... Break!

PART I

GETTING TO WORK

Part I looks at the growing trend of male plastic surgery, what procedures are topping the charts, and what types of men are getting what kinds of surgery and why—the answers may surprise you.

CHAPTER 1

REAL GUYS, REAL RESULTS: WHAT IS THE DADDY DO-OVER?

Guys have hectic lives. For most of us, we struggle just to stay on top of our jobs and keep our businesses going, all while trying to devote an equal amount of time and energy toward our families. If there's any time or energy left, we try to devote it to ourselves, but that rarely works out.

Take just trying to exercise each day. I know that if I miss a morning workout, then I'm never going to make it up. I could tell myself all day long that I'm going to work out at four o'clock, for instance, but then something happens with the business, or a patient comes in at the last minute, or I have to pick up one of my four kids early from school. Any number of things get in the way, and after a few years of that, you discover that your pants aren't fitting the way they used to, your chest is starting to resemble a woman's, and you constantly look tired.

That's the reality, and as much as we may tell ourselves we're going to hit the gym more or eat salads for lunch, the fact is that most of us don't, and even those who do still struggle with the physical impacts of too little sleep and the inevitabilities of aging and gravity. And with that loss of physique comes the loss of self-confidence, so we care less and treat ourselves worse, and it becomes a self-perpetuating downward spiral.

It used to be that the only guys I saw in my practice were the ones who were dragged in by their wives. The women would come in for a Mommy Makeover (the title of my first book, released in 2015), and once they saw the results, they'd bring their husbands in, saying to them, "Look, you can't keep showing up to work looking like this. You've got to be more put together. Do some maintenance."

Now it's different—men are coming in on their own. They understand the benefit that erasing the effects of aging has, not only on their confidence, but also on their career. They've seen the aftermath of their colleagues not only being passed over for promotion but being caught in the "reorganization" of their newly acquired company. While the corporation won't dare say it had anything to do with appearances, when the comparison with who didn't get "downsized" is made, the results are obvious. Young, virile, energetic are the dominant themes. Like it or not, without these descriptions added to the mix, words like "experience," "expertise," and "proven track record" mean "Old Man," and may lead to career downfall.

This is why the Daddy Do-Over exists; it's plastic surgery, also known as cosmetic surgery, to help restore a guy's physique—and consequently his confidence. Through the Daddy Do-Over, I've played a part in helping guys make a positive choice for themselves and their family, simply by restoring their confidence.

A Daddy Do-Over may include some or all of the following procedures:

1. A **gut tuck** to tighten up the stomach and remove excess fat.

2. **Liposuction** to remove stubborn fat around the stomach, love handles, and other areas that are either challenging or impossible to reduce through exercise alone.

3. **Breast reduction** to flatten out and eliminate man boobs.

4. **Hair transplant** to restore your natural hairline

5. **Neck lift or Kybella injections** to restore that sharp angle to the masculine chin.

6. **Botox** to get rid of those extra crow's feet and the "11" lines between the brows, and fat transfers to improve the wrinkles around the nose, mouth, and even lips.

7. **Buttock augmentation,** because even guys like their pants to stay on sometimes.

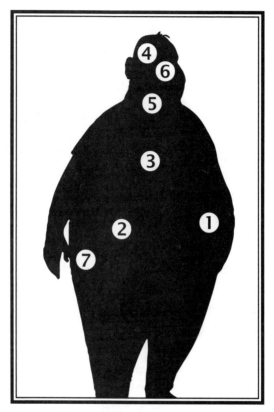

Figure 1: The Daddy Do-Over is plastic surgery to help restore a guy's physique—and in the process, his confidence.

If the corporate risks aren't enough, I have heard the horror stories of the dad being tossed to the curb because the wife chose the pool boy. We've all seen our buddies' devastation when finding out about their wive's infidelity and second-guessing themselves with the "what if" questions. If they'd only taken better care of themselves, the "personal trainer" wouldn't have been able to sneak into their territory. Caught up in a messy divorce, now they have to reinvent themselves so they can get back on the market.

Alternatively, if we're in the middle of a midlife crisis and we think we need to look outside our marriage to prove that we've still got game, let me save you a shit-ton of trouble. Forget the expensive sports cars, or the even more expensive mistress on the side. Consider spending money on yourself. Plastic surgery can help you make the changes from *outside in* to give you that boost of confidence needed not only in the boardroom, but also in the bedroom.

Guys, if you're reading this book, you've likely reached a point in your life where you need a little help in getting your natural confidence back to its highest level. If you think plastic surgery is only for celebrities and flabby dads, I can tell you thousands of stories that say different. But let me share just a few with you now.

PLASTIC SURGERY IN ACTION: EX-ATHLETES AND COPS

Take the former NFL player who came in for a specific problem that he was tired of dealing with. He'd played on the offensive line—this guy must have been at least six-foot-seven, 330 pounds. Despite his imposing size, he got made fun of for man boobs. He did every-thing he could to cover them up, including heavy, heavy workouts, really beefing up the muscle to try and overcome it.

Of course, he didn't just target the condition. He worked out his whole body and got himself to where he could play in the NFL. But even then, there was still this fatty bit of breast tissue that remained. He covered it some when he was playing, but after he retired, he didn't work out like he used to, and the condition became a lot more obvious. Finally he decided he'd had enough and came to see us. If you're prone to gynecomastia, even if you have 4 percent body fat like he did, the problem will likely persist. You can't lose it with extra weight loss or cover it over with exercise. Plastic surgery was his answer.

A seasoned police officer came into our office for the same reason. He was in good shape, but he couldn't wear his flak jacket because of the pain it was causing from rubbing against his nipples. He couldn't stand it. He was in constant pain, but it's not like you can take pain meds and wield a gun. He dealt with the pain for years, but it meant taking days off, and the department finally threatened to put him on disability. He wasn't the kind of guy to live off of the state. He was doing good things and providing for his family and wasn't going to accept disability, so he found us.

We had another guy who was dragged in by his wife because he was too embarrassed to take his shirt off in public. He'd lost a bunch of weight, but the leftover skin was sagging and he was particularly embarrassed about his chest. He ended up needing a more extensive surgery than some others, including a nipple transplant to bring everything back to where it needed to go, but after that procedure he was like a new person. He came into the office after his surgery with a whole new confidence. He felt and looked more masculine, walking with his shoulders back and exuding his masculinity and confidence.

Guys from all walks of life have come in over the years for different procedures, from a fire chief who needed a gut tuck after losing weight because he was just tired of excess skin hanging over his pants, to athletes, lawyers, judges, salesmen, marketing directors, contractors, and models. We've helped all types of guys for all types of reasons, both functional and cosmetic. And the results aren't just physical—there's a huge psychological benefit as well.

THE COMPETITIVE EDGE NO ONE'S TALKING ABOUT

Confidence is one of those make-it-or-break-it states, especially with guys. Depending on what kind of job you have, your personal level of confidence could make all of the difference in whether or not you're assigned the best accounts, sign the best clients, or close the biggest deals. It's something that you naturally project, and it's the cumulative result of your emotional state—your confidence in yourself—and your physical appearance.

Research conducted by the National Bureau of Economic Research has found that attractive people make more money,[3] and additional studies have pointed to a combination of good health, intelligence, attractiveness, and other factors such as a "winning personality" as drivers for higher salaries.[4]

Facial first impressions are a big deal in the business world because, let's face it, if you look like you've spent years eating fast food, hanging around the bar, and generally not taking good care of yourself, the instant connotation is that you're sloppy, lazy, and can't get the job done. Who's going to trust a multimillion dollar sale to someone who can't seem to get organized enough to plan his meals ahead of time or hit the gym at least a few times a week?

In reality, of course, that person may not be lazy at all. It could just be genetics and years on the road taking its toll, but the visual first

3   Daniel S. Hamermesh and Jeff E. Biddle, "Beauty and the Labor Market," American Economic Review 84 (December 1994): 1174-1194, http://www.nber.org/papers/w4518.pdf.

4   DiSalvo, David "Science Asks: Do Pretty People Really Make More Money?" Forbes, February 21, 2017, https://www.forbes.com/sites/david-disalvo/2017/02/21/science-asks-do-pretty-people-really-make-more-money/#7d0a9c82dbd6.

impression is that they're losing their edge. And that has an impact.

At the same time, there's also the threat from the younger generation moving in with their own brand of confidence. They're fit, single, and act like they can take on the world. And while you may have all of the experience, again it comes down to that first visual impression—does the client want the vital go-getter to throw their boundless energy into their project, or the guy who looks experienced but frankly a little worn out?

That's where we see guys starting to come in—to restore that competitive edge. They may just be looking for a slight reduction in frown lines, or an eyelid lift to make them look younger and more alert. Or they may just want to add a little definition around the chin to restore that connotation of strength and masculinity that a strong chin projects.

We had a C-suite sales exec come in for just that reason. He was pretty athletic and had these massive arms and chest. But, even his friends called him "biceps," no matter what he did, he couldn't get rid of his big hanging chin. We ended up doing three rounds of Kybella—an injectable treatment that destroys the fat cells under the chin—and he did great. His chin ended up more chiseled with a more defined jawline, and he's much more confident because of it.

In today's culture, youth and beauty are prized more than ever. Men don't want to be left in the dust, but to keep up, they have to balance projecting their wisdom through age and experience while also portraying youthful energy, virility, and confidence.

THE RAW STATS

Then there are the raw statistics. In 2015 alone, men accounted for more than 1.2 million plastic surgery procedures—9.5 percent of the total done that year, which is an increase of more than 325 percent in cosmetic procedures among men since 1997.[5] In 2016, the popularity increased by another 3 percent, to greater than 1.3 million plastic surgery procedures performed on men.[6]

Top surgical procedures performed by plastic surgeons for guys in 2015 included:

➜ Liposuction (51,370)

➜ Nose surgery (30,928)

➜ Eyelid surgery (30,696)

➜ Male breast reduction (30,464)

➜ Facelift (13,726)

Male breast reduction surgery alone has gone up by 173 percent since 1997, with a 26 percent increase just in 2015.

Nonsurgical procedures have increased with men, as well. More than 447,000 botulinum

5   American Society for Aesthetic Plastic Surgery, "2015 Cosmetic Surgery National Data Bank Statistics," 2015, http://www.surgery.org/sites/default/files/Stats2015.pdf.

6   American Society for Aesthetic Plastic Surgery, "2016 Cosmetic Surgery National Data Bank Statistics," 2016, https://www.surgery.org/sites/default/files/ASAPS-Stats2016.pdf.

toxin procedures—which includes Botox, Dysport, and Xeomin—were done on men in 2016, as well as more than 341,000 skin rejuvenation procedures. And while liposuction was the top surgical procedure in 2015, the fifth most popular nonsurgical procedure for men was nonsurgical skin tightening, which includes evening out stubborn conditions such as love handles and refining jowls.

THE DADDY DO-OVER: A HEALTHY WAY TO REACT TO A MIDLIFE CRISIS

Then there's the emotional factor. While confidence is a combination of mental state and physical appearance, the biggest emotional factor when it comes to considering plastic surgery is in men confronting a midlife crisis.

It's something we all hit—some of us multiple times—and the stereotypical response is to get a mistress, get a sports car, or go do something else really stupid. Why? Because we don't feel as young, we've lost a lot of our confidence, and we're not sure if we still have "it." We try to prove something to ourselves by doing all these idiotic things, and in the end we just make a mess. There's a cost to all of these things, not all of which is monetary, and they all have significant negative impacts down the line.

When you hit that emotional wall, you have a choice. As the head of the family, you have a duty to live by example. Are you going to show your children that the answer to a receding hairline is a one-night stand? Or that only a mistress or a wildly expensive sports car can make you feel better about your fading looks? The cost of these midlife crisis Band-Aids is far more than just monetary: Are you willing to forever throw away your dignity in your son's eyes? And is this how you show your daughter how a "real man" acts? These decisions may also mean the loss of your respect and potentially the loss of your family. So, why not do something instead that will positively impact you and consequently your family, and help you feel more confident at the same time? Don't throw it all away—instead, invest in yourself.

Midlife crises are all about facing your mortality. You don't have to give up and give in. You can still appear as youthful and virile as you feel. You can still go out and do things with your kids and not be embarrassed at the pool. Instead, you can take off your shirt, show off your muscles, and then lift up your kids and throw them around the pool like they're begging you to, because you're confident in how you look.

Sometimes all it takes is a little help getting rid of that one stubborn area of fat to kick-start a healthier lifestyle, which is more important than ever as you age. One of the reasons our mortality becomes more real to us around this time is that those annual visits to the doctor are becoming a bit more ominous. Blood pressure may be up, cholesterol counts aren't great. The doctor may pinch a love handle or two with a raised eyebrow and remind us about those fun reality-check stats, such as how a waist size over forty inches leads to a significant increase in morbidity and mortality.[7]

You're at a much higher risk for suffering a heart attack with a waist size over forty, and as for morbidity, the heavier you are, the more strain is being placed on your joints and the harder it is for you to move around. You might not be able to bend down and pick up your daughter as easily, or get on the ground and play cars or Legos with your son, because your joints just can't take it. Do you want to leave your daughter to walk down the aisle in her wedding dress by herself because you were too lazy to get healthy?

Plastic surgery isn't meant for total weight loss, but it can be used as a springboard to better your health, encourage further

7   Harvard T.H. Chan Obesity Prevention Source, "Waist Size Matters," accessed 3/7/17, https://www.hsph.harvard.edu/obesity-prevention-source/obesity-definition/abdominal-obesity/.

weight loss, and maintain your results. Or, as a reward for hitting the gym, such as to get rid of those love handles that are stubbornly covering up your abs. It's a lifestyle change that can be facilitated with the right procedures.

Ultimately, with the Daddy Do-Over you're increasing your health and increasing your confidence, and it might actually reignite that spark in your marriage. Your wife might look at you a little differently, and you can start having a more positive outlook on the world in general. By helping your health and confidence, you're avoiding those other midlife crisis disasters and instead keeping your family together and even strengthening your bond with them because you believe in yourself again. You have "it"—you just might need some help to see it again.

CHAPTER 2

THE MALE DILEMMA

Plastic surgery is a different story for men than for women, and that's mainly because of something we call the Male Dilemma.

When it comes to aging, men have it much easier than women. Men are admired for their "distinguished" look—a little bit of gray and some wrinkles are respected, whereas those same qualities in women aren't held in as high regard. When it comes to the business world, appearance is considered important for both men and women. Successful businesspeople don't show up to a board meeting dressed for the beach with their beer belly hanging out. No one would take them seriously. But looking "put together" isn't exactly a walk in the park for guys. For instance, it's not as acceptable for men to look like they took an hour or two getting ready every morning, and to be honest, most men don't have that kind of time or patience. We want to look put together, but not too together, and all without the extensive effort.

This is where the Male Dilemma lies. How do you make yourself look professional and composed without spending a lot of time pulling it off? How do you take care of yourself without "looking" like you do? How do you look complete without looking "over done"?

THE MALE DILEMMA AND PLASTIC SURGERY: KEEPING A NATURAL LOOK

With male plastic surgery, the key is to avoid anything that looks too polished or manicured. There has to be some roughness around the edges to make it appropriate. And, depending on your lifestyle, different procedures and approaches may apply.

No matter what procedure we're doing, we're going to want to keep a natural look. With guys, that means taking a nuanced approach. With facial rejuvenation, for instance, we're not going to completely take away the crow's feet or round out the chin; we're going to keep the character of the face.

> **NO MATTER WHAT PROCEDURE WE'RE DOING, WE'RE GOING TO WANT TO KEEP A NATURAL LOOK. WITH GUYS, THAT MEANS TAKING A NUANCED APPROACH.**

When looking at the face, we don't just look at one specific area—we look at the entire canvas and examine how one aspect plays into the next. Visually, we divide the face into thirds: (1) the eyes and forehead, (2) the middle area around the cheeks and nose, and (3) the lower third of the jowls, chin, and neck. Then we look at what we'll need to do to progress toward the patient's ideal result.

For example, you don't want to end up with great looking eyes but a saggy face and turkey neck. You want to do little bits to each part, making subtle changes along the way. Say you do a little around the eyebrows and crow's feet one time, then a touch of filler followed by some skin care and micro-needling to the mid-face the next time. You can do Kybella around the chin, or another nonsurgical avenue for neck tightening, and maybe some skin tightening overall that's not drastic—just enough to bring up the loose skin and restore some youthful vitality.

And this doesn't all need to be done within a short, strict time frame, either. It can be just a little here and there over the years, just to keep you on top of your game. In fact, the newer trend, which I totally agree with, is maintenance. Doing small amounts more frequently, as opposed to waiting for a total overhaul, allows for a more subtle intervention to be chosen and allows for less noticeable, more natural results.

Even when we consider the chest and abdominal area with men, a nuanced approach is still applicable. Yes, we typically want more of an overall change to occur, especially when considering the gut tuck or excision of man boobs, but the approach is still very much individualized to the specific circumstances of each patient.

CHAPTER 3

GOLFERS, DADS, GROOMS, AND BUSINESSMEN— WHO IS PLASTIC SURGERY FOR?

Although not every guy will fit into the next few categories, the following are several of the top male lifestyles that we often see for plastic surgery, along with the procedures that work best for bringing back that youthful vigor while not looking "over done":

THE CONFIDENT DAD LOOK

There's a little joke in my family about who gets Botox. My wife typically gets it because—as she's pointed out—I've got to be the disciplinarian for the kids, so I have to be able to give them the stink eye as needed. Thankfully, I don't have to do it that often, but eventually we realized that I could do with some Botox, too—I didn't need to have that stern look on my face all the time. The stern voice is usually enough to get the point across.

For your typical dad, sometimes all it takes is a little bit of wrinkle reduction and some definition around the jaw to restore that youthful look and confidence. Other times, dads will come in for procedures so that they can keep up with their wives, or to augment an area they've been working on particularly hard at the gym.

Popular procedures for dads include:

→ Botox *(see page 298)*

→ Filler *(see page 154)*

→ Kybella *(see page 209)*

➜ Facial rejuvenation *(see page 135)*

➜ Gut tuck *(see page 237)*

➜ Liposuction *(see page 255)*

➜ Gynecomastia elimination
    (see page 215)

RUGGED: TIME IN THE SUN

Whether it's from hiking the Rockies, surfing every summer, or playing eighteen holes every weekend for thirty years, prolonged unprotected sun exposure can have serious effects.

Years ago, we didn't know that sunscreen was so important, but today we're seeing the results—from leathery skin, to premature aging, to skin cancer. These days we know enough to wear sunscreen, but for those of us who are dealing with the after effects of sun exposure, there are several options for treatment:

Non-invasive procedures:

→ Skin care regimen *(see page 140)*

→ Hydrafacial *(see page 145)*

→ Micro-needling *(see page 147)*

→ Neurotoxins like Botox
   (see page 148)

→ Facial fillers *(see page 154)*

Surgical rejuvenation to the...

→ Forehead/eyebrows *(see page 180)*

→ Eyelids *(see page 176)*

→ Face *(see page 135)*

→ Jowls *(see page 157)*

→ Mouth *(see page 156)*

→ Neck *(see page 164)*

SKIN CARE, SUNSCREEN, AND SMOKING

I try to be a barometer for what guys will and will not tolerate, which means I practice what I preach. Medical-grade skin care regimens, for instance, can be a twelve-step process every day, but I don't know a single guy who will tolerate that—myself included.

When I recommend a treatment like skin care, I tailor it to the condition we're looking to treat. If it's sunspots, for instance, we can narrow the treatment down to a few steps to help fade them, and then prevent them with sunscreen.

The most important thing I recommend to any guy who spends even a little time in the sun, however, is to use sunscreen. Not only are you preventing eventual skin damage and potential skin cancer, but you can tell the health of a person by the health of their skin. A healthy individual has more buoyant skin, while an old man has thin, crepe-papery skin that looks sunken and decrepit.

Smoking, too, has a rough impact on your skin. Not only is it harder for your skin to repair damage from smoking, but the decreased blood flow caused by nicotine both thins out the skin and ages your face prematurely, in addtion to making it harder for wounds to heal. And don't think that vaping is any better for your skin. In fact, it may actually be worse because the toxins are simply broken down into even smaller particles, which can permeate further into your skin and lungs.

Of course, as an occasional cigar smoker myself with friends who smoke a lot more than I do, I know that cutting down or eliminating your smoking is easier said than done. But even limiting it can have a positive effect. Just keep in mind that the longer you go without some sort of correction to your skin, the harder it will be to get results.

Though smoking has a large impact on your overall appearance, a subtler culprit of rugged, worn down skin is the sun.

LEAVE THE "SQUINTY LOOK" TO THE WESTERNS—FURTHER EFFECTS OF THE SUN

Along with skin damage, all that squinting in the sun—especially if you aren't wearing a hat—results in more activation of the muscles around the eye, leading to more crow's feet and potentially impacting or extending the drooping aspect of the eyelids. This can make it look like you're half asleep, even when your eyes are wide open.

Between the eyes, too, gets more of a workout and can result in more-defined "11" lines in what's called the glabellar area. Options for these conditions range from Botox to fillers to surgical eyelid lift procedures. Regardless of which procedure is done, the approach is going to be different than it would be for a woman, because there are some anatomic differences in a guy's face. For instance, guys typically have a bigger, broader nose than women, with thicker skin. Our cheeks are a little bit flatter and wider, too, so when we're putting filler in, for example, we're careful not to round out those features too much; just reduce the wrinkling and keep those sharp features in play.

THE STRONG BUSINESS EXEC LOOK

The business world is fierce, and staying ahead of the competition today often takes a lot more than just smarts. You've got to look the part, too.

When a lawyer client of mine came in for the first time, he said the reason he made the appointment was that he didn't want to look like he couldn't "hang" anymore. He wanted to still be with the younger crowd, but he also needed to maintain that edge of experience. It's a fine line, but once you cross it, a lot of business execs feel like they've lost that competitive edge.

It's a matter of visual first impressions.

A 2016 *Men's Health* article, for example, reported that when researchers tracked women's eye movement on the beach, the first thing the women tended to look at on men were the abs, followed by the face, then the arms and shoulders.[8] On the street, where the men were fully clothed, they looked at the smile, height, hands, and overall style.

Another article found that factors such as confidence and overall appearance were some of the first things women noticed about men. For example, one poll respondent stated that "If he doesn't care about his appearance, he probably doesn't care about maintaining most things in his life." Another wrote, "I think attractiveness is so

8   Ali Eaves, "The Very First Thing Women Notice About Guys," *Men's Health*, May 7, 2016, http://www.menshealth.com/sex-women/the-very-first-thing-women-notice-about-guys.

linked to confidence. It makes so much of a difference."

When it comes to confidence in particular, one of the leading visual indicators of confidence in men is a strong jawline, maybe because of the evolutionary edge. According to a study published in scientific journal, *Evolution and Human Behavior*, a man's lower jaw tends to be both wider and longer because it "would have been useful during his long ancestral history as a hunter." For instance, the enlarged openings of the nose, mouth, and jaw would have allowed for enhanced airflow, making it easier for the male to keep up an adequate supply of oxygen "required for the efficient use of his larger muscle mass."[9]

These qualities obviously don't have that same survival relevance today, but the genetic inclination to believe that a male with stronger facial qualities is more likely

9   Victor S. Johnson et al., "Male facial attractiveness evidence for hormone-mediated adaptive design," *Evolution and Human Behavior* 22, no.1 (2001): 251 – 267.

to survive—or in today's world, succeed—remains. It leads to a competitive edge in sports, in obtaining a mate, and in the competition of business.

Additionally, an article in *New Spirit Journal Online* found that "a prominent chin indicates a strong sex drive.[10] The size of the chin directly correlates to the level of the male sex hormone testosterone in the body. In other words, the larger the chin, the more testosterone, and thus a stronger sex drive."

It all goes back to those hardwired genetics—the procreation aspect. People find more symmetrical faces more attractive for this same reason. Nature makes things in symmetry, which leads us to believe that the more symmetrical something is, such as a person's face or full physique, the more likely they're going to have longevity and the ability to reproduce, compared with those who are slightly unnatural—asymmet-

10   Haner, Jean, "Signs of Sexuality in the Face," *New Spirit Journal Online*, April 11, 2015, http://newspiritjournalonline.com/signs-of-sexuality-in-the-face/.

ric—because they're genetically less likely to survive.[11]

This is why we spend a lot of time at our office working to create symmetry. It's usually a subtle issue, but if you just need, for example, a little touch of filler here or Botox there every few months or once a year, that's got it covered for most guys. It's a short, quick solution to some of those asymmetry problems that may be holding them back.

Ultimately, appearance—and your confidence in your appearance—is not only important for the opposite sex, but also relates to our level of success. Attractive people are often more successful, get paid more for what they do, and are better at making the sale. If they're slovenly, unkempt, and can't tuck their shirt in because their belly is in the way, they're a lot less likely to win over a client than the guy who's cut and in shape. It's that subconscious, evolutionary inclination

11   Gillian Rhodes et al., "Do facial averageness and symmetry signal
      health?," *Evolution and Human Behavior* 22, no.1 (2001): 31-46.

that—although we can deny all we want— still strongly exists in the human psyche.

Procedures that business executives most often consider include:

➜ Botox/Protox *(see page 298)*

➜ Filler *(see page 154)*

➜ Kybella *(see page 209)*

➜ Facial rejuvenation *(see page 135)*

➜ Gut tuck *(see page 237)*

➜ Liposuction *(see page 255)*

➜ Hair restoration *(see page 165)*

➜ Hair removal *(see page 172)*

➜ Beard augmentation/ transplantation *(see page 171)*

➜ Gynecomastia reduction *(see page 215)*

GROWING YOUNG TOGETHER

An attorney came into our office once at the request of his wife. She'd had a few things done, and after seeing the results, she'd turned to him and said, "Okay, buddy. It's your turn. What are you going to do?"

We've had wives just schedule an appointment for their husbands, too, where the guy walks in with a slightly confused look on his face, saying, "She just told me to show up here. I don't know why, but I was told to be here, so help me out." And we do, we help him out with his appearance, and a lot of the time they tell us later that the treatments and/or procedures also helped with their marriage.

It's not always the wife telling the husband to come in, though, or dragging him into the office kicking and screaming. Sometimes we see couples in friendly competition with each other, with one coming in for a procedure, followed shortly thereafter by their partner, who gets the same procedure and then one-ups it with an additional procedure or treatment. Other times, we have the couple come in as, well, a couple. They could be a younger couple preparing for their wedding, for instance, or an older couple wanting to look good for a second honeymoon or an anniversary trip, so they'll both get a little liposuction in different areas, say around the legs for her and on the love handles for him.

Whether they're in it together or in a friendly competition, the more popular procedures for couples are:

➜ Botox *(see page 298)*

➜ Filler *(see page 154)*

➜ Kybella *(see page 209)*

➜ Facial rejuvenation *(see page 135)*

➜ Gut tuck *(see page 237)*

➜ Liposuction *(see page 255)*

BACK IN THE SADDLE: DIVORCEES BACK ON THE MARKET

When it comes to being a divorcée, the challenge is basically in selling yourself again. You're back on the market, potentially after having become comfortable with letting yourself go a little bit and slipping into a more passive routine. If you think about before you were married, for instance, you were doing what you could to keep in shape. And when you got engaged, you were doing what you could to get fit and keep up with your wife for the wedding day.

But then all that time passed, and suddenly you're back on the market and you realize that you've got to get back in the game. You can't just throw a picture of yourself from fifteen years ago on your online dating profile—that might work to hook the first date, but how impressed are they going to be when they meet you in person?

Where plastic surgery can come in is in helping you figure out the best thing we can work on for your overall appearance, whether it's hair transplantation, skin care, tightening up the area around the eyes, or working on the chest or abdomen.

In the end, what you decide to do often depends on what will make you feel the happiest and most confident, and what you are looking for in a mate. For instance, some women find older men attractive, so getting back in the game may just be finding out how to keep that aspect of experience while building on those qualities that emphasize virility and strength.

When it comes to being a divorcée on the market, you're not just selling some product or widget; you're selling yourself. So how are you going to make what you have the most attractive or the best possible product? You don't go sell a car with all your chips and garbage in the trunk. You go and get it detailed. You make sure it looks its best, and the same should go for you as you hit the dating scene.

At the same time, I also recommend that guys getting ready to hit the dating scene after a long period of married life consider getting their "insides" checked before we start working on the outside. Plastic surgery isn't going to "bring her back" or make you irresistible. Instead, it might be smart to speak with a professional before getting any work done just to make sure your expectations going forward are healthy and that you're comfortable with entering the dating world once again.

SECOND-TIME DADS

Whether you lost your first spouse through divorce or unexpected circumstances, when you do find the right person the second time around, the exciting and challenging part is that you may wind up with a younger wife, which often leaves you feeling one of two ways:

1. you want to keep up with her and not be the old guy sticking out like a sore thumb in the crowd, being mistaken for her father, or,

2. if you have kids together, you don't want people mistaking your son or daughter for your grandkid.

Just like anything you have for a long period of time—a house, a favorite car—your body is going to need some maintenance from time to time. A car will need new tires, for instance, and a house will need a new roof. Your body is going to need upkeep as well, and just like a house and a car, those improvements are often long-term investments. And they're something that you can have control over.

Of course, you can't control when you run over a nail in the road or a tree limb falls on your roof, just like you can't control when some aspect of your genetics kicks in and you can't get rid of that double chin or fatty breasts. But you can have some control of your own appearance by taking preventive measures such as using sunscreen, stopping smoking, and improving your diet and exercise.

Where plastic surgery comes in is in helping you gain more of that control back, helping you with that chin or chest, and potentially reversing some of those aging effects, as well.

For second-time dads and divorcées, preferred procedures include:

➜ Facial rejuvenation *(see page 135)*

➜ Botox *(see page 298)*

➜ Eyelid lift *(see page 176)*

➜ Kybella *(see page 209)*

➜ Filler *(see page 154)*

➜ Hair transplantation *(see page 165)*

THE DAY SHE'LL REMEMBER FOREVER

Your wedding day is one of the biggest days of your life, and likely the one day when you'll be photographed more than any other time in your life.

Regardless of whether or not you're a first-time groom or if it's not your first rodeo, there are some things you can do to make sure you're looking your best for those lifelong pictures.

Procedures popular with grooms:

- ➔ Botox *(see page 298)*

- ➔ Filler *(see page 154)*

- ➔ Kybella *(see page 209)*

- ➔ Laser hair removal *(see page 172)*

- ➔ Liposuction *(see page 255)*

Typically, what we see with grooms-to-be is more maintenance work—some "manscaping" before the big day. We'll do some hair removal around the eyebrows, for instance, or the chest. We're also seeing a lot with Botox to soften out some of those wrinkles and that harshness in appearance around the face. Occasionally we'll see filler, if they want to augment their cheeks or their square chin to get a little more of a chiseled look. And if they're honeymooning somewhere like the beach, they may want to uncover those abs with a little liposuction, just to get rid of that fatty covering.

The most important thing when it comes to surgical procedures such as liposuction before the wedding is to give yourself about three to six months to see final results after the surgery, as you're going to have some residual swelling. A good way to plan for this is to schedule any surgical procedures about the time your fiancée is picking out her wedding dress.

FATHER OF THE BRIDE/GROOM

We had a bride-to-be come into our office, dragging her father in with her to get fixed up before her wedding. She pretty much led the appointment, telling us, "He needs to get this fixed. He needs liposuction and he needs some Kybella. Let's get this going."

And he did. He got liposuction and a couple other things done, which I thought was admirable. I realized, as the father of one daughter and three boys, I'm going to do everything I can to make her day special. I won't want to ruin it by showing up all sloppy and fat and embarrassing at her wedding. I'll embarrass her with the way I dance—that should be enough.

We're now seeing a lot more wedding parties come in that will do a series of treatments as a group. Whether it's the bride coming in with her mom or the groom bringing in his groomsmen party, they'll all agree on doing a few procedures just to get "cleaned up," so to speak, before the big day.

Procedures popular with father of the bride/groom:

➜ Botox *(see page 298)*

➜ Filler *(see page 154)*

➜ Kybella *(see page 209)*

➜ Laser hair removal *(see page 172)*

➜ Liposuction *(see page 255)*

BABY BOOMERS

There's been a huge increase in the baby boomer population recently at our practice, mainly because they're not aging the same way their parents did. They're not hitting age sixty or sixty-five and just hanging up the hat. These days, sixty is the new forty, and sixty-plus-year-olds are staying a lot more active. They're traveling, living longer, and even starting new careers in their retirement. Because of this, we see a lot of baby boomers coming in and saying, "Look, I don't want to look like a shriveled up old granddad. I still want to be seen as a guy who's 'got it.' What can you do?"

One guy in his early sixties told us about his dad who lived to be ninety-five and always regretted that he never did anything to get rid of his turkey neck. His dad lived with it for thirty years before he died, he told us, and he didn't want to wind up the same way.

With the baby boomer crowd, the more popular procedures include:

- ➜ Botox *(see page 298)*

- ➜ Filler *(see page 154)*

- ➜ Eyebrow surgery *(see page 180)*

- ➜ Eyelid surgery *(see page 176)*

- ➜ Rhinoplasty (nose surgery) *(see page 193)*

- ➜ Facelift *(see page 160)*

- ➜ Hair transplantation *(see page 165)*

- ➜ Liposuction *(see page 255)*

CHAPTER 4

KEEPING IT REAL: WHAT PLASTIC SURGERY IS AND ISN'T

Having realistic expectations about your Daddy Do-Over is crucial for being happy with the results, especially in the long run, which is why it's important to know what a Daddy Do-Over *can't* and/or *won't* do for you.

➔ **It's not going to make you look fake.** When it comes to guys, we're very careful about preserving the aesthetics of the male anatomy. We're not going to feminize your appearance or make you look plastic-y. Facelifts aren't like they used to be, for instance. We're not yanking it all back to get rid of every line and wrinkle. The goal is to keep the normal contours of your face and just refine what's needed.

➜ **It will not make you homosexual, heterosexual, asexual, or metrosexual.** It will not change your sexual orientation. Plastic surgery changes your outside appearance, and, yes, we hope it affects your inner self-confidence, too. But the rest of your desires, attractions, and so on will not be affected, except that you might feel more virile after improving your confidence. So, just because you have plastic surgery, your sexual orientation will not change. (There are plastic surgical procedures available for those looking to undergo gender reassignment surgery. These are highly specialized and complex surgeries that I currently do not perform. If interested, I recommend visiting a board-certified plastic surgeon in your area that you can find at www.plasticsurgery.org.)

➜ **It *can't* save your marriage.** If your marriage is already strained, going through the surgery won't help and might even put more stress on your relationship. I always discuss this aspect with my patients. If you're trying to look like the ripped twenty-something running around at her gym, that won't happen. That's not a good motivation for surgery.

➜ **It will not make you irresistible.** Plastic surgery may change your looks, but it won't change your personality. While outward appearance is what initially attracts a mate to you, in order to sustain any sort of relationship, you have to treat people the right way. If you're a jerk, after plastic surgery you'll just be a better-looking jerk.

➔ **It's *not* weight loss surgery.** A gut tuck is meant to get rid of an overhang, not remove large amounts of abdominal fat. Before I do a gut tuck, I recommend that you be within 10 percent of your ideal body weight—that's where you're going to have the best results. Liposuction only removes small amounts of body fat in select areas. Of course, losing weight is easier said than done, and some just can't ever get there; sometimes guys will choose to go through the surgery a little bit before they get within 10 percent of their ideal weight. The results can still be good, if not excellent, and some patients are willing to accept that limitation.

➔ **It's *not* magic.** You're trying to look and be the best that you can be. I can't turn you into somebody else.

➔ **It *won't* turn the clock back twenty years.** A Daddy Do-Over can do a lot to bring your body closer to a healthy ideal and give you a more youthful appearance, but we can't make you look like you're a teenager again.

Plastic surgery is best in subtleties, especially with guys. Men often don't have the ability to tolerate a lot of downtime, so drastic changes are usually neither wanted nor warranted. Typically, these procedures are just to augment what you have—to give you a sharper jawline or younger looking eyes, or to help make that six-pack visible again. Even if the treatment or procedure isn't as noticeable to everybody else, it's typically a beneficial change that helps you feel that much more confident.

And sometimes, when it comes to confidence, you have to fake it until you make it. In jobs such as sales, for instance, if you're switching over to a new job, the only thing you may have going for you at first is your confidence, and your overall appearance plays a huge role it that. If your clothes fit well, if there's no excess skin or fat hanging out, and your face has some of that youthful, go-getter vibrancy to it, you're much more likely to start landing deals.

WHO SHOULDN'T GET PLASTIC SURGERY

There are certain conditions that put men (and women) at higher risk for complications, especially with riskier procedures. Many times, clearance from a primary care physician and/or maximization of your current medical conditions will be indicated in order to mitigate some of the risks associated with surgery. However, there are still some men who should consider avoiding plastic surgery altogether.

- ***Severe heart trouble:*** Patients with this condition may not be able to withstand any level of anesthetic and should have surgery only if needed in an emergency. This is elective surgery, after all. I want to have successful results with a good-looking and "alive" patient. It does neither of us any good if you end up after surgery as a good-looking corpse.

- ***Uncontrolled diabetes:*** This can lead to prolonged healing and extensive wound-healing problems.

- ***Chronic smoker who can't/won't quit:*** Smoking—and, more specifically, the nicotine in the cigarettes—decreases the caliber of the blood vessels that are so desperately needed in the healing process.

- ***Chronic blood thinner usage:*** While the thinner blood may be good for you on a day-to-day basis, I like my patients to be able to stop bleeding after an incision.

- **Unrealistic expectations:** This is true surgery, with real downtime. To expect an immediate result after surgery is not realistic.

- **Noncompliant individuals:** Some men are used to only giving orders in their life—at their job, in their home, etc. You have to understand that I give you recommendations based on my experiences of what I have seen work and work well. If you are unwilling to give up some control for a while and follow these recommendations, your results will suffer, we will not get along well, and I don't want you as my patient.

- **Negative attitude about plastic surgery:** For the Daddy Do-Over, this is elective surgery. Even though your wife or significant other may have brought you in and encouraged you to seek treatment, at the end of the day, it is your body and your appearance that we are working on. You have to be able to look in the mirror and be happy with the choices you have made. Many times, all this takes is a bit of education about the aging process, procedures available, and the specific options recommended for your circumstances. If you are completely against taking care of yourself and bettering your appearance and your life in general, you will not do well. I will not operate on these individuals.

- ***Looking for the quick fix:*** Plastic surgery is meant to fit *into* your lifestyle, not make up for it. If you are going to continue treating yourself like garbage and not take care of yourself, your plastic surgery will not last, it will not be worth it, and I will not be a part of it. I encourage all of my dad patients to make healthy choices so that they can be around for their families for a long time. A Daddy Do-Over can be a part of this lifestyle, which also includes a healthy diet, frequent exercise, and maintenance of their appearance.

THE FAT OF THE MATTER

As I said above, plastic surgery isn't for massive weight loss. We can help with love handles and get you more defined abs, but lipo isn't going to totally disintegrate that beer belly. In fact, fat removal, especially around the belly, is a different situation between women and men.

Women tend to carry that fat more externally, whereas guys carry it more around their internal organs in a form we call visceral fat. And this kind of fat can't be helped by plastic surgery at all. In plastic surgery, we have to stay well above the organs, which means that the visceral fat can only be worked off by diet and cardiovascular exercise.

Think of one of those guys out there—or you may be one of them—with a big barrel chest or a beer belly, but when you push against that chest or belly, you hit hard muscle, not soft fat. That's because the fat is behind that muscle layer, around the organs where we can't get to it. When we try to compress the midsection with a gut tuck, we can only go so far in because the excess fat pushes back out against us.

Another way to look at it is as to think of wearing a jacket that's three sizes too small, shoving a beach ball inside of it, and then trying to zip it up. You can only compress that beach ball so much before you break the zipper—in other words, have difficulty closing up the skin during the gut tuck surgery.

WHAT'S THE TYPICAL AGE OF MALE PLASTIC SURGERY PATIENTS?

There's no specific age that we start seeing adult male patients. Some guys start showing up in their mid-twenties for some Botox here and there, typically right around their "11" lines. Or we'll start them on a skin care regimen—just low-maintenance steps such as a facial wash and sunscreen that can help them keep that youthful appearance longer.

The patients in their mid-thirties and forties are often looking for a little more—maybe doing a couple more areas of Botox, getting it between the eyes but also on the forehead and around the crow's feet area. Others will start to get that sunken, hollowed-out look between their eyelids and cheekbones, so they'll go with a little bit of filler instead of going right for the surgical eye lift. The filler helps especially in that it kicks the need for eyelid surgery down the road a few years before you're ready to do a surgical correction.

By the mid-to-late forties and early fifties, we see guys still doing a lot of the same things, but maybe covering a little more surface area or using a stronger dose of toxins, skin care, or sunscreen. Guys already need a stronger dose of toxins such as Botox and Dysport because their skin tends to be thicker than women's, and/or the muscles there are stronger, so as they age they may be using double what a woman would need to create subtle changes in a particular area.

HOW YOUNG IS TOO YOUNG FOR PLASTIC SURGERY?

Anyone who has a teenager at home is painfully familiar with the attitude of "Hurry up, I have to have [fill in the blank] now or the world is going to end." They may begin asking for plastic surgery because they think their nose is too big for their face, or their ears are too big, or any number of things. It seems like the end of the world to them, and yes, there have been a few one-off instances where we've done plastic surgery for younger patients due to bullying issues, but overall, our recommendation is to wait.

And when they throw a fit, I tell them that I had the same problem.

Growing up, I had an enormous nose that did not fit the size of my face. To paint you a picture, I not only had this giant nose, but I also had a mullet and an earring, acne and braces, all while growing up in New Jersey. You think I didn't get bullied?

It's tough being a teenager, but often the best thing to do is to wait it out. You grow into things. It may take until your late teens, even early twenties, but believe me, you'll likely eventually even out. It took a while for me, but I finally grew into my nose without needing any kind of surgery.

When it comes to those one-off instances, however, there have been a handful of times where it was incredibly beneficial to a younger teen to undergo plastic surgery. In one case, we had a young kid who was a soccer player, in great shape, and a good athlete, but he was suffering from gynecomastia, which was making life difficult for him both physically and mentally. We were able to reduce those for him and he did great.

Even still, I put the kid off for a year before we actually did the procedure, because we wanted to see if he would grow into it. But it just became too much of a problem. He wasn't doing as well as he should have in many different areas of his life, both socially and athletically. He couldn't take his shirt off if his team was playing shirts and skins, for instance, and he wouldn't go to the pool in the summer with his friends because he was too embarrassed. So we finally decided to go with the breast reduction surgery.

In another instance, we had a kid whose father challenged him to lose a certain amount of weight by his graduation, and he did. In all, he lost close to a hundred pounds with diet and exercise, working out like crazy to reach his goal. The problem was, though, that once he lost all that weight he was left with all this floppy skin hanging off of him that wouldn't spring back into place. So his dad said, "You know what? You don't need to live like this the rest of your life just because you were slack on your diet for a few years as a teenager." So, as a reward, he brought his son in to have the excess skin removed.

Each case we see is individualized, but my first question when we see younger patients is always going to be, "Is this something you can grow into?" Teens, and teenage boys in particular, are still growing at sixteen or seventeen, so we don't want to do a procedure such as breast reduction and then, at nineteen, the kid hits a growth spurt, fills out, and everything would have been fine. They're called the awkward years for a reason, so as a rule of thumb we tend to wait until the late teens before considering any type of surgery, particularly around the face, where the nose and ears often take the longest to grow into.

As a surgeon, I can guide you through what is appropriate and safe, as well as what can be done in a single surgery versus multiple surgeries. As you think through the possibilities, I can help you process and envision what the end result could be. Then we can discuss what Daddy Do-Over procedures are right for you.

SET ASIDE THE PRIDE AND GET YOUR SH*T FIXED

I've said it before, but I'll say it again because it deserves repeating: We're guys—we don't like to admit we need help. The old stereotype of a guy driving five hours in the wrong direction because he wouldn't stop for five minutes and ask for directions exists because it's true. We think we can do everything on our own. But the fact is, we can't.

We can hit the gym six days a week and do all those exercises until we're blue in the face, but sometimes that little problem area just isn't going to go away without surgery. You may be able to mask it, like the NFL player we talked about earlier who worked out enough to cover up his gynecomastia for years, but you're not going to solve it. Sometimes it's just genetics. So it's okay to give up your pride and admit that there's something you can't do. It doesn't make you any less of a Superdad. And then you can learn about all the options you have for what you *can* do, and your pride will come back. You're not giving up your masculinity by going to a plastic surgeon. In fact, whatever you end up choosing to do is likely going to lead you to feel *more* masculine, more confident. Add to that the reality that (1) plastic surgery is much more commonplace these days, (2) you can get it done privately, and (3) the stigma is slowly easing, and you're left with no excuse. Don't let your pride get in the way of doing something positive for yourself.

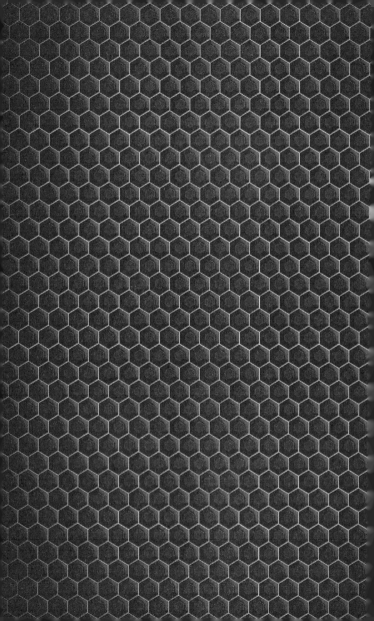

PART II

PREP WORK

Getting ready for your Daddy Do-Over is just as important as the decision process and even the surgery itself. If you're well prepared, you'll get through the recovery period faster and with a lot less stress. In this section, I'll explain all the logistics of what you need to consider in advance.

CHAPTER 5

CHOOSING THE RIGHT SURGEON

One of the most important decisions you have to make before having a procedure involves choosing a skilled and accredited plastic surgeon. This can be a bit confusing at first, because many doctors offer cosmetic procedures and many consider themselves cosmetic surgeons. However, *a cosmetic surgeon and a plastic surgeon are not the same*. While it's true that all plastic surgeons are cosmetic surgeons, the reverse is not true.

Plastic surgeons are trained in cosmetic and reconstructive surgery of the face and body (some are facial plastic surgeons only). A cosmetic surgeon may have a completely different kind of training. According to the American Board of Plastic Surgery (ABPS), a board-certified plastic surgeon must have a minimum of five years of residency training in all areas of surgery, including at least two years devoted entirely to plastic surgery. To become board certified, the doctor must then pass comprehensive written exams (four hundred questions) and oral exams (where a panel of experienced expert surgeons grill you to make sure everything you do in and out of the operating room is appropriate, safe, and ethical). If you want to know more about the certification process or to see if a surgeon is board certified, check the ABPS website at www.abplsurg.org.

Cosmetic surgeons are not necessarily plastic surgeons. Cosmetic surgeons are physicians of any specialty (like OB/GYN or emergency medicine) who have taken a course (often over just a weekend) in cosmetic surgery. So why does this matter? According to the American Society of Aesthetic Plastic Surgery (ASAPS), physicians who call themselves cosmetic surgeons could be trained in any specialty, including a nonsurgical specialty; it is very unregulated. Just as you wouldn't want me, a plastic surgeon, to do a cardiac catheterization for you, you wouldn't want your cardiologist, who calls himself a cosmetic surgeon, to do your gut tuck. If you stick only to plastic surgeons board-certified by the ABPS, you'll almost certainly end up in good hands.

> **IF YOU STICK ONLY TO PLASTIC SURGEONS BOARD-CERTIFIED BY THE ABPS, YOU'LL ALMOST CERTAINLY END UP IN GOOD HANDS.**

MORE THAN TEST SCORES

After confirming your surgeon is board certified, you want to make sure that the surgeon has plenty of experience. As a general plastic surgeon, I am thoroughly trained in plastic surgery and am not confined to just one area of the body. You want to ensure your surgeon has dealt with issues at least as complex as your own, and more complex is even better. There are some good ways to research this.

WEBSITES

Browse through many websites to see which doctor's style makes you feel most comfortable. Look at the verbiage on the web pages to determine how they speak to their patients. Look at before and after pictures of the surgeon's work and try to find a patient with similar characteristics to yourself.

REFERENCES

Check online for patient reviews to ensure that the surgeon has plenty of satisfied patients. If possible, try to speak with former patients of the doctor you are considering. Be cautious of surgeons who won't allow this—ask yourself if they are trying to hide something. Patients will likely give you the unabridged version of their experience. I am pleased to say that our patients give us very high marks and tend to refer their friends. For me, there is no stronger compliment than a personal referral from a satisfied patient. I love it when some of my former patients take the opportunity to share their Music City Plastic Surgery experience with someone new and encourage them to experience us for themselves.

CONSULTATION

The next step is having an initial consultation with the surgeon. When you first visit the surgeon, you shouldn't feel rushed or get the impression of a giant mass-production machine. You should feel free to ask the surgeon anything, including details of his or her training and experience and what the surgery will cost. If you don't perceive a good connection with the surgeon, or if you don't like any of his or her answers, it may be time to interview someone else. I often find that patients have talked to several doctors before deciding to work with me—and that's just fine. I especially like informed patients who have made a conscientious choice.

THE MUSIC CITY PLASTIC SURGERY EXPERIENCE

In my practice, I want to treat people exactly the way I would want to be treated. My goal is to deliver an unparalleled plastic surgery experience. I want my patients to look and feel their best, in hopes that with this new confidence they will make a positive impact on the lives and relationships of those around them. While you may initially feel a bit awkward and uncomfortable as we begin, we hope you will quickly begin to feel you can trust everyone in the office as we aim to make your experience as positive and stress-free as possible.

My staff and I want to deliver great care, from the moment you call for the first time all the way through your last postoperative visit and beyond. It's an unwavering commitment to excellence to ensure we take care of whatever you need to get your work done.

Since Daddy Do-Overs can address any part of the body, from the face to the wedding tackle, I make it a point to ensure that my patients understand all of what they're about to do. That thorough education is an aspect in which I take great pride. I always talk to my patients as individuals first. I want to get to know them, where they're coming from, what's bothering them, and what they'd like to change. I listen very attentively to what my patients tell me. Only after establishing that trust do we get to the nitty-gritty of what needs to be done.

Most initial consultations take approximately an hour, just to make sure we're both on the same page about what you're looking to achieve—now and ultimately over time.

CHAPTER 6

PRE-OP QUESTIONS AND CONCERNS

The younger and healthier you are preoperatively, the easier time you will have with recovery postoperatively. While many objections can be made about why *not* to have plastic surgery now, I believe in living life to the fullest. If you look at yourself in the mirror and don't like what you see, do something about it. There is never the perfect time to have surgery. Life happens. Work will always be crazy—kids will still have school, homework, and after-school activities, and completing that "honey do" list will continue to drift away just out of arm's reach.

The timing of plastic surgery involves many factors, including your age and overall health, your life circumstances, and your financial situation. We'll continue to cover these considerations in this book, but my overriding thought is that if most of these factors line up, why wait? You deserve to enjoy a better body now.

But let's not get ahead of ourselves. Let's delve deeper into some of the other concerns I have seen most of my patients face when making these decisions.

IS IT SAFE?

The usual procedures for any Daddy Do-Over are very safe. (See part 3 for specifics of the individual procedures.) If you have a skilled surgeon working in a modern operating room, complications during the surgery are very rare. From my experience, most of the guys we see are relatively young and healthy without serious medical problems. And by "relatively young," I mean that the thinking today is that sixty is the new forty. So, forty is really young—and so is sixty. Those factors

> **SIXTY IS THE NEW FORTY. SO, FORTY IS REALLY YOUNG—AND SO IS SIXTY.**

make the surgery and healing process much easier on the body. A healthy guy can certainly go through several procedures at once and make a good recovery. This doesn't add much to the length of the surgery or the time you're under anesthesia. We jokingly ask our patients, "Why waste a good general anesthesia on only one surgery?" The additional pain and healing time isn't much greater either—approximately two to three weeks separately and only slightly longer when combined. Most prefer to have that downtime just once. There's also no long-term detriment to your system in undergoing chest and stomach procedures at the same time.

A lot of patients are surprised to learn that they can do multiple procedures at once. Many come to the office with preconceived notions that only one problem can be fixed at a time due to the safety, pain, or recovery time. After we discuss it, however, most patients choose to go for a combination of procedures. They understand that they're going to have to make a lot of arrangements for work, home, and so on—and they'd rather have to do that just once. Plus, doing the procedures separately also means going through the preparation and downtime more often. And why pay the hospital operating room and facility fees more than once?

ADVANTAGES OF COMBINED PROCEDURES

➔ Single anesthetic (may be safer)

➔ Single downtime

➜ Similar pain

➜ Arrangements (work, kids, house, etc.) only once

➜ Potential savings (anesthesia and facility fees)

MENTAL AND EMOTIONAL IMPACT

Whether you opt for one or multiple procedures, it's also important to note that plastic surgery also has its share of side effects—some good and some more challenging. Some points to consider:

➜ The transformation in your self-image—you'll feel more self-confident, leading to good things in your life and your career

➜ The responses of those around you to your decision—some will congratulate you, and some will question you

➜ The potential impact on relationships—some will be pleased for you, some will be critical or even jealous, and some relationships may even be reinvigorated

And, although more common in women, it's not uncommon for my male patients to have some mood swings (or take a ride on the emotional locomotive) as the surgery date approaches. Especially the night before, they may think, "What am I doing? I just need to hit the gym harder. Why am I doing this surgery? What if something goes wrong? Who's going to provide for my family? I'm doing all of this for my ego. I don't need more defined abs. I don't need this flab of skin cut off. This is ridiculous." Usually this involves giving up some control, which most men abhor. There is the potential for a short-lived bout of depression in the initial postoperative phase with some procedures as well.

Feeling anxious or guilty before an operation is perfectly natural. Second thoughts and doubts are normal. But you're doing this for *you*, and it's very, very safe. As I tell my patients, you're much more likely to get into a car accident on the way to the hospital than you are to have any problems during or after the surgery.

THE MONEY QUESTION

Plastic surgery treatments and procedures cost real money, but they're not indulgences or a sign of being selfish. It's an investment in yourself—one in which you'll reap the rewards for the rest of your life. A better way to look at this may be not, "What does it cost?" but rather, "How much is it worth to you?" How many times do you look in a mirror and think, "I wish I could get this taken care of?" How much is it worth to look in the mirror every time for the rest of your life and feel good about yourself? Would you pay a penny each time? If you would, then you've probably already covered your investment.

Let's look at this in a slightly different manner. Let's look at ROI (return on investment). We have all heard about the studies that show that attractive people earn more compared with unattractive people. We discussed earlier that some women consider a man's best feature his confidence.

We can play the credit card commercial here a bit. If this newfound confidence after losing the man boobs can give you the cojones to approach that drop-dead gorgeous model, and you two fall in love and get married, what is the ROI?

→ Male pattern breast reduction surgery (no more man boobs): $10K

→ Two weeks downtime off work: $5K

→ Confidence-induced approach to meeting and falling in love with the woman of your dreams: priceless

Or maybe a little less dramatic:

→ Surgery cost: $10K–20K

→ Two weeks downtime off work: $5K

→ Confidence gained and finally demanding the salary you're worth/increased sales: $10K–20K/year × X years. (Within the first year, that may already be a 100 percent return on investment, and it only continues to pay forward.)

→ Increased ability to close sales (assume increase in year prior sales of $50K–100K with endless chain of referrals) = infinite ROI!

And don't worry about not having all the money up front. My office staff works with our patients to finance their surgery. There are many good options here. Some people put it on a credit card and get the bonus miles or points. Some specialized lenders will finance it—we can help set that up for you. The companies work with you on the repayment terms. Because Daddy Do-Overs are planned for and scheduled in advance, you know up front what it will cost and when the payment is due. This total cost includes surgery, follow-up, anesthesia, and facility fees. (To explore the financing option that works best for you, visit www.musiccityplasticsurgery.com/financing.)

TALKING TO THE KIDS

If you have kids, which a lot of our male patients do, talking to them about your upcoming procedure is something you may choose to ask your wife to do, or do in tandem with her. You can also do it on your own, but your wife may be more empathetic in explaining how you won't be able to do as many things for a couple of weeks, and she can also show the kids her support for what you're about to go through. Depending on their ages, there may be some additional challenges to discuss with your kids when it comes to plastic surgery, like how to maintain a healthy body image for themselves (more on this below). This can be a little tricky, because you want to be honest with your kids but not scare or worry them. We have found that what you say depends mostly on their age.

Many of my patients have kids in the five- to nine-year-old range. For kids at that age, you can tell them the basic, limited truth. Say something like, "Dad is having an operation, and he won't be feeling well for a couple of weeks." That's usually about all young kids want or need to know. One of my patients told his eight-year-old son, "Dad is having a doctor fix his stomach." When the boy asked why, he replied, "Because the doctor said so." The response at that point was simply "Okay." Another patient of mine told his son he wouldn't be able to throw the ball with him for a couple of weeks because of an upcoming procedure. They made a plan to watch some games together on TV while he recuperated, and no "dad time" was missed.

For older children, you might give more detail and explanation. In my view, we need to be very careful about discussing plastic surgery with our children. As they grow up, we want them to have a positive body image. How Dad carries himself and his views on his physical appearance and that of others has a strong impact on his children. Our kids need to know that cosmetic surgery isn't necessary to be attractive. They need to know that you're having surgery not to become a different person, but to restore your body and to look as good as you feel.

Older teenagers can be an additional support system for Dad, as well as for Mom and the family, helping to keep it all together and even instructing the other children. Sometimes when we challenge our children, we are pleasantly surprised at how they can rise to the occasion.

CHAPTER 7

GAME PLAN: PREPARING FOR SURGERY

Dads are a lot more involved with their families nowadays than they used to be. Not too long ago, Dad was the patriarch and did what he pleased. When he came home, he'd sit in his Barcalounger while Mom cooked up dinner, and then he'd eat and go back to sit down and read the paper or watch the news.

Those days, for the most part, are gone. Today's dads are doing much more stuff with the kids, taking them to after-school sports practices or even coaching their teams, cheering them on at the ball field, and taking them on camping trips. It's a team effort, as both Mom and Dad are more likely to be employed full time and often share the responsibilities at home. Because of this, when it comes to working out a pre- and post-op game plan, it's wise to find someone to help take care of the kids, such as the in-laws or some close friends, especially if you're expecting your wife to be taking care of you. That way, you don't have to be worried as much about being interrupted during the early days of your recovery.

LOGISTICS

Whether you have two working adults in the house or your wife is a stay-at-home mom, you'll need to plan out your schedule at work and at home well ahead of time. If you have a family trip coming up, for instance, you'll want to have any surgical procedures completed a good three to six months beforehand to allow yourself enough time to heal. You're not going to want to be lifting heavy luggage or carrying a sleepy youngster with incisions that are still healing.

Remember, this stuff is real surgery and it takes real recovery time. You're not going to get a procedure done one week and then be ready to roll the next. We always recommend at least two to three weeks of healing time before traveling in any capacity. We want to make sure you take the time to actually heal as best you can, but mainly this is also to avoid the risk of blood clots, as the time span between days five and fourteen is when these are most likely to occur.

Additionally, you'll need to consider the potentially awkward social downtime, when it might be uncomfortable to show up at social events with bruises from a facelift or eyelid surgery. These will also fade after about three weeks, but you might want to avoid attending public functions or giving big presentations until then.

PRE-OP PLANNING

Let's look at a timeline for a typical Daddy Do-Over surgery. Once you decide that you want to proceed, we usually schedule the surgery for a few weeks out. That gives you enough time to:

➔ Get a preoperative checkup by your primary care physician.

➔ Organize payment.

➔ Schedule to have someone who can help you with personal care for at least a week. (And if you have kids, there's only so much your wife is going to be able to do. If you think you'll need more help, consider reaching out to relatives or hiring a short-term caregiver.)

➔ Make arrangements at work.

➔ Take care of any home prep—such as scheduling carpools for school drop-offs/pickups that you typically help with, working with your kids' friends to arrange rides to after-school practice, arranging for meal delivery services if you typically take turns making meals, etc.—making sure to get everything set up as far in advance as you can.

PLAN SURGERY FOR WHEN HELP IS AVAILABLE

Along with arranging for child and household care, you will need some assistance of your own during the recovery period. That's a reality you need to plan for carefully. A lot of my patients arrange to do their surgery during a slow time at work for them and their wives. Some of my patients have seasonal businesses and do the surgery in their off-peak period. I had one patient recently who saved up some extra vacation time for his surgery. When he went back to work, everyone said to him, "You look great! Your vacation must have been awesome!" Many spouses arrange to take a few days off to help out. That's why we do a lot of surgeries on Tuesday or Thursday—the spouse takes a few vacation days and can also be home to help through the weekend.

> **I HAD ONE PATIENT RECENTLY WHO SAVED UP SOME EXTRA VACATION TIME FOR HIS SURGERY. WHEN HE WENT BACK TO WORK, EVERYONE SAID TO HIM, "YOU LOOK GREAT! YOUR VACATION MUST HAVE BEEN AWESOME!"**

Especially during the first days of your recovery period, you need an adult nearby to help you with things like getting out of bed, going to the bathroom, and getting dressed. If you've had a gut tuck, for instance, one of the challenges is getting in and out of bed properly. We teach you how to do it so that you don't strain, but having some help is still very important. If you've had chest work done, your chest muscles will be sore and you won't want to use them much. You might also have a drain in place in your abdomen or chest for a few days. That takes a little management. After surgery you'll also be wearing a surgical garment to hold things tightly in place. Getting that on and off is a bit of a challenge at first—some of my patients have likened it to "putting a sausage back in its casing" or putting on a "full body condom"— so you'll want to have someone help you.

This one is especially important: while you're recovering, *you can't lift anything heavy*. You also won't be all that quick on your feet. While you're taking pain medications, you're not allowed to drive, and once you're off the meds, driving may still be mildly uncomfortable for a while. If you do any of these things, you might hurt. To me, these are reminder pains that say, "Okay, you shouldn't be doing this. You need to slow it down."

If your spouse can't help much, this may be the time to ask friends and family members to pitch in. I say this with a little hesitation, though. Think this through carefully and be choosy about whom you invite. You want this time to be restful, not more stressful because someone "other" is in the house. You want it to be someone both you and your wife (and your kids) are completely comfortable with and can communicate clearly and honestly with. Remember that your emotions (and those of the kids) can be a bit on edge; be sure that your helper is someone you can all feel supported by, not someone who might present additional challenges of their own.

We have found that the best people for this type of support are people who already know you and your family well (though hiring a private nurse just to take care of you isn't a bad idea, either). You won't mind if they see you at your worst (physically and emotionally), when you haven't taken a shower and you're groggy and grumpy. Choose those who are most likely to step up and help out when you are most vulnerable.

I have had patients who take the other approach and hire a private nurse whom they've never met before. The potential advantage of this is the feeling of anonymity with a stranger. If this person, who you don't know, sees you at your worst, who cares? You'll likely never see them again. It gives some guys freedom to react however they will naturally after surgery and on pain medication, without feeling guilty or having to worry about being embarrassed later by their actions. Sometimes, avoiding this extra stress can help a guy heal quicker and more comfortably. If you are unsure of which is right for you, use your best judgment and ask your wife. If she's anything like mine, she'll tell you.

CHAPTER 8

TOUGH AS NAILS: PLANNING YOUR RECOVERY

POST-OP: AT HOME RECOVERY

While you are recovering, set your expectations appropriately. Don't set yourself up for failure. Things are *not* going to go perfectly—no matter how much planning was done ahead of time. If you have kids, you're used to plans going awry—there are some days when you're falling back on plan D or E, not just plan B, before lunchtime. But this is not the time to be dragging yourself around trying to keep up with every-one's needs. All that stuff can wait. It really can. Trust me—I'm the father of four children and am married to another doctor. We do fine with just one parent around for a bit, and if Dad can use the excuse of, "Mom's out of town," or "Mom's under the weather," as a reason for pizza every night for a week, then so can Mom. The two of you can talk about how it's okay if veggies aren't on the dinner plate for a few days and how everyone will certainly survive on easy meals for a while— it's just one less stressor for her to deal with.

As guys, we like to think the world revolves around us and that the family will flounder without our direction at all times. In reality, your family is probably very similar to mine and thrives on the female presence. My boys like to remind me how much more they love their mother than they do me. So if you're not actively involved in their lives for just a little while, they'll still be okay.

It's also a good idea to keep in mind that your recovery period can be a good lesson for your kids on how to be strong even when you're hurting. For boys, it's an opportunity to show them that you don't have to be this stoic man who doesn't show emotion. At the same time, though, you don't want to be a crybaby who's overreacting to everything. Instead, just be honest and say, "I'm hurting a little bit here," or, for the younger kids, "Daddy doesn't feel well," and just keep it somewhat vague without overreacting in either direction.

POST-OP: OUTTA SIGHT, OUTTA MIND

Here's another suggestion: avoid the chaos altogether. The bustling house and the noise of the kids tend to be the main reasons why many of my patients escape to a hotel for a few days after the surgery. If Dad can't bear the chaos of the home, we now have special accommodations (with the rare addition of nursing care) at a few local hotels for our postoperative patients. A beautiful room, no noise, room service, no temptations to get out of bed and do yard work or play with the kids or tell them to settle down so you can rest. No need to wake the sleeping monster and have you act in a way you might regret later. And, no guilt from staying in bed all day watching the games on TV if you can't hear the kids in another room. Out of sight, out of mind means better recovery. Just remove yourself from the situation (physically, mentally, or both) and concentrate on yourself. The lawn can wait … really!

GUYS ACT TOUGH...UNTIL IT COMES TO PAIN

Remember, you don't always have to be the tough guy when it comes to pain. It's okay to admit it when something hurts. Ultimately, it may mean that you end up healing quicker— if you can get in front of the pain, instead of trying to be all macho and tough until suddenly you're whimpering in the corner, curled up in a fetal position because you waited too long to do something about it. Take your medication. That's why we gave it to you. Then wean yourself off of it after a day or two.

That said, plastic surgery is not as painful as it may sound. We're not usually going through muscles or deep down into body cavities, which is where a lot of the pain comes from in other surgical procedures, such as hernia surgery or appendix removal.

For instance, with liposuction, whether it's for gynecomastia or elsewhere, we're basically taking a stainless steel straw and riding along the muscle layer to take out the deeper layer of fat above. The result is that you feel like you've been punched in that area a few times. It's more of a soreness, as opposed to the sharp shooting, ripping-through-muscle type of pain that other surgeries may involve.

Pain in plastic surgery tends to be more of an inconvenience and soreness than anything else, like you worked out too hard on one area and you're regretting it the next day. With gut tucks, for example, we're tightening those muscles and reorienting them forward, so afterward it may feel like you did a whole bunch of sit-ups. Usually, any incisional pain with surgery is fairly short lasting and can be handled with just a little bit of pain medication.

> **PAIN IN PLASTIC SURGERY TENDS TO BE MORE OF AN INCONVENIENCE AND SORENESS THAN ANYTHING ELSE, LIKE YOU WORKED OUT TOO HARD ON ONE AREA AND YOU'RE REGRETTING IT THE NEXT DAY.**

But pain is subjective. In a strict comparison between men and women, men do not handle pain nearly as well as women. So even though we think we're a hell of a lot tougher, when it comes to surgical pain and dealing with procedures and needles, guys tend to fall way below women when it comes to pain tolerance.

Take laser treatment, for instance. It's commonly known that women can take hundreds to thousands of pulses from laser treatment, which feels like little shocks, while men can typically only take about three to five and then they're done. We're far removed from the level of pain that women can handle, so we need to stay aware of that as we plan our recovery.

POST-OP SMORGASBORD

When it comes to what you should and should not eat or drink after outpatient surgery, I leave a lot of those decisions up to the patients.

In the early phases of coming out of anesthesia, some patients will wake up and the first thing they want is a hamburger. Others can't even stand the sight of crackers and ginger ale—it all depends on your reaction to the anesthetic. The longer procedures, of course, often result in stronger reactions, but a lot of advancements have been made in anesthetic use in the past five to ten years. So when some patients say to me, "I had surgery twenty years ago and I was deathly sick," or, "I was vomiting for three days straight," I tell them that those days are gone.

Today, we don't need to use as much or as strong of an anesthetic. Even if it's a longer outpatient procedure, we don't have to give you as much medication to keep you comfortable, and you typically end up going home that same day. I tend to do a lot with local anesthetics, augmenting that with a light general anesthetic. The general anesthetic is kind of like turning the lights on or off: either you're totally awake and aware, or you're completely out.

Other options include IV sedation, which has the patient sitting on the fence between awake and completely out, and MAC, or monitored anesthesia care, which feels kind of like you've had a few drinks and just don't care. Local anesthetics last longer—about six to eight hours—and act like a nerve block, which can help with recovery.

When it comes to eating after any surgical procedure, the initial food aspect really depends on (1) the anesthetic, and (2) the procedure.

If we tightened you up with a gut tuck, for instance, then your stomach capacity may not be the same because it's being compressed, so you need to keep that in mind. If it was just lipo, however, you may feel more comfortable with a larger meal.

On the other hand, with facelifts, if we're tightening the jowls, lifting everything and keeping those muscles in place, that strength layer suddenly becomes tighter around the face, and the ability to open your mouth wide is limited for a while. So we say "no aggressive eating" after these procedures, like biting an apple or digging into a triple decker burger.

Hot and spicy foods, too, should be avoided, as they may conflict with the pain medications and with the anesthetic, or they may just upset your stomach during early recovery at a time when you could really do without the heartburn or those gas cramps.

What you *should* have, though, is at least *something* with your pain medication, even if it's just a glass of milk, as the medicine can wear away at the lining of the stomach. Milk will help prevent that erosion, so even if you don't feel like eating, a glass of milk is a good idea. However, it's important to note that as a source of nutrients, milk alone is not substantial enough to promote healing.

While you recover, it's important to ensure that you are getting enough protein. Protein allows you to rebuild the layers of your body that were incised during surgery. Think of it as building a house. You need the protein to repair the walls of your body's physical defense layer (i.e., your skin) like a builder needs the drywall and spackle. Lean meats and fish, nuts, and even post-workout protein shakes are healthy options for getting protein during your recovery period. And if you run into any constipation issues—another unpleasant side effect of pain meds—let us know and we'll recommend some over-the-counter medications to help with that.

SO, WHEN YOU SAY LIMIT ALCOHOL ...

You'll want to *avoid all alcohol* while you're taking pain medication. Mixing it can lead to severe complications, specifically respiratory depression, where your body no longer has the drive to breathe.

It's also not a good idea to mix prescription pain medication with over-the-counter pain medication, because a lot of the prescription pain medication has a combination of

Tylenol or Advil intermixed with the narcotic, and overdoing medications like acetaminophen can lead to liver damage, liver failure, or even death.

So start with your prescription, and work your way off of it before switching to something like extra strength Tylenol, and stick with water for a while, as well as liquids containing electrolytes to help keep your fluid intake up. You'll be feeling better soon enough, and safely celebrating with a drink or two before you know it.

THE EMOTIONAL LOCOMOTIVE: EMOTIONS AND WHAT TO DO WITH THEM

We spoke earlier about the emotions you may experience before a surgery, and that locomotive doesn't stop after you come out of the anesthesia.

I call this the emotional locomotive because it can start slowly, build up steam, and then seem to get out of control like a runaway train. As we add fuel to the fire by being pissed off, grumpy, or tired, this ride on the crazy train can be tough to get off of. In practice, many guys either don't notice or just ignore this situation as it gains momentum, until it is like a true locomotive going full steam ahead. We can get all fired up and then blow our stack.

SSED OFF
RUMPY
IRED

THE EMOTIONAL LOCOMOTIVE

In the early postoperative period, this emotional locomotive of mood swings and short-term depression (or unmasking of sub-clinical depression) are common. Often this will manifest itself as tiredness, grumpiness, and just not feeling like yourself. Men will often express emotions such as rage or frustration significantly more than other emotions such as depression.[12] As your surgeon, I can assure you that this is perfectly natural—the locomotive will run out of steam, and your emotions will soon return to normal.

But let's take a minute to explore why this happens.

Although it's difficult to point to a single exact cause, many factors impact how you feel after a surgical procedure. Surgery is a significant physical stress to your body: general anesthesia is used, narcotic pain medications are prescribed, and steroids may be used, all of which can throw off your

---

12   Margrit Bradley, "Emotions—Differences Between Men and Women," HealthGuidance, accessed December 4, 2017, http://www.healthguidance.org/entry/13971/1/Emotions—Differences-Between-Men-and-Women.html.

hormone balances. Pain may interfere with sleeping and deplete your body's reserves, leaving you feeling tired and worn down. I believe you heal more quickly when you are not in pain, because your body devotes the resources to healing and not fighting pain, so I encourage use of the pain medications, at least in the first few days. However, for some, the anesthesia and pain medications can also alter sleep patterns.

Stress also plays a big role in how you deal with the postoperative period. We already mentioned the physical stress of surgery, but the mental stress of the impending surgery, and then waiting for the final outcome, plays into your mood as well. Often with surgery, especially facial surgery, you may look worse before you look better. Seeing the swelling, bruising, and temporarily raised or reddened scars may leave you second-guessing why you voluntarily chose this. Try to keep this in mind while you heal.

GETTING BACK TO NORMAL

While these stressors are very real, the important thing to understand is that they can be minimized with a little planning and preparation. This emotional turmoil often ends on its own, with just a little time.

Here are a few suggestions:

→ **Time alone:** Some guys just need space to deal with it on their own. Let your spouse know ahead of time that this may be the case so there are no hard feelings if and when this does occur. This will be different than her instincts of talking things out, so preparation on both sides of this will be key.

→ **Get outdoors:** Go for a hike, check out the backyard hammock, or just try to spend a few minutes outside in the sunshine.

→ **Shower:** Typically, a shower is allowed after two days. This goes a *long* way toward patients feeling like themselves again.

➔ **Eat healthy:** Fruits, vegetables, and good protein intake speed recovery and provide your body with antioxidants to fight off stress.

➔ **See your doctor:** Schedule a visit to your plastic surgeon so that he or she can update you on the healing process and potentially alleviate some anxiety.

➔ **Use your computer responsibly:** There's a lot of junk health information on the Internet. Visit ASPS, ASAPS, or www.realself.com for some positive feedback and stories about plastic surgery.

Remember the time frame for healing from surgery. Many times, full results are not realized for a few months. Give your body the chance to heal before you second-guess your decisions. We'll discuss the specifics of each procedure in the following chapters so that you will be well prepared and informed when it's time for your surgery.

PART III

PROCEDURES

Now comes the fun part: delving into the **solutions** to our problems. Most men will jump to this section because we are doers— we want to solve the problem and now. **Part 3** covers the surgical and nonsurgical interventions available for your Daddy Do-Over.

Plastic surgery for guys differs tremendously from plastic surgery for women—from what aspects you're looking to preserve or enhance, to what you can and can't do when it comes to more extensive procedures such as gut tucks and liposuction. In the following section, we'll look at several surgical procedures specifically from a "for guys" perspective, and take a closer look at exactly what each option will involve. If you have more questions, you can always check out our website at www.musiccityplasticsurgery.com, give us a call at (615) 567-5716, or drop by for a private, confidential consultation.

CHAPTER 9

FACIAL REJUVENATION

Dave was a middle-aged VP of sales at a fairly prominent national firm. By all accounts, he was a good-looking guy, but his years were starting to show. Even though he was one of the most successful VPs, he noted that he wasn't getting assigned to the bigger accounts as frequently anymore. He mentioned that the company seem to be "grooming" one of the newer associates and this guy was taking the world by storm. "With my experience, I can easily work circles around this guy, but when I look in the mirror I see this old guy staring back at me," he told me. He wondered out loud if his boss saw the same thing and assumed he wasn't physically up to the demands of the bigger accounts.

After an examination, we decided on a treatment plan together. We started slow with him but did enough to offer the subtle but profound impact—subtle in that no one but he and I knew, but profound in that he looked much more refreshed and renewed. He planned for his series of treatments, but he started to experience significant changes after his first Botox session. And not just in his looks. Along with the gradual shift in his appearance, he started to notice the impact it had at work. Instead of keeping quiet when the new accounts were assigned, Dave had a renewed confidence to "request" these accounts. As he recalled during one of his now regular treatments, "My boss looked me over and I could just see the wheels turning inside his head as he correctly deduced that I *was* physically up to the task. The funny thing is, the only thing that changed was the way my face didn't appear as harsh and weathered anymore."

The better part of the story is that with his renewed confidence and increased productivity at work, Dave's marriage seemed to improve as well. It may be because, like most of us guys, Dave derives a good chunk of his identity from his career. When his confidence in that portion of his life was low, it affected other areas as well. It's a self-perpetuating cycle that feeds on itself both negatively and—thankfully in Dave's case and for many other men—positively, as well. I'm not sure it was only his visit to my office that caused the change (Dave tells me, "You saved my career, my marriage, my life"), but it does go to show you that a Daddy Do-Over *can* improve your performance in the boardroom ... and the bedroom.

When it comes to faces, the male facial structure is typically broader and wider than the female. The chin and jaw are wider, the chin is stronger, and the forehead is more pronounced, all of which contribute to a stronger, wider, broader, more masculine look. Because of this, we want to make sure we keep or augment those masculine features when doing facial rejuvenation in guys.

EGG OF YOUTHFULNESS

Our faces show aging through either sun damage, deflation, or descent, and often by all three. One way to look at it is with a helpful analogy (as first suggested to me by Washington, DC, plastic surgeon William Little) that I use with a lot of my facial rejuvenation patients: the Egg of Youthfulness.[13]

Think of a youthful face like an egg, with the fat side up and the narrower side down. As we age, that egg turns over, with the fat side eventually sitting on the bottom and the narrower side on top, and everything

13   FaceliftDC, "Dr. Little's Philosophies," accessed December 4, 2014, http://faceliftdc.com/dr-littles-philosophies/face/.

drifting downward. Eyelid bags start to develop. There's deflation and descent along the cheekbones, and the jowls form. The eye sockets, too, begin to go through a reabsorption of the bone, which widens out the orbital rim and causes the skin just below the eyeball to droop down and sometimes bulge out. The cheekbone may begin to lose bone mass as well, leading to some flattening of the mid-face, which contributes to the signs of aging.

The youthful buoyancy of the face is gone, and sun damage begins to affect the superficial layer of the skin, leading to fine lines and wrinkles, with further deflation and descent of fat, tissues, and skin contributing to the deeper wrinkles of the face. I'll show you how to turn the facial egg to youthful side up, but first let's look at some avenues for improving our faces from outside in.

SKIN CARE

Believe it or not, as of 2015, male skin care products represented a $3.4 billion market in the United States alone.[14] This means that more men are paying attention to their skin and taking preventive measures instead of allowing the sun to wreak its havoc.

Before considering any kind of facial procedure, including Botox or fillers, the best thing you can do for your skin is to get on a skin care regimen. A lot of those little spots or moles that pop up on your skin over time due to sun exposure can be taken care of with medical-grade skin care. And I don't mean the goop you find in department stores or at hair salons or online. I mean the strong, medical-grade solutions that penetrate deep enough to actually have an effect on the physiology of the skin, as opposed to just changing things up top.

---

14   Rochelle Nataloni, "Male Aesthetic Niche," *The Dermatologist* 23, no. 8 (2015): http://www.the-dermatologist.com/content/male-aesthetic-niche.

Apart from sun protection, skin care also helps with the hydration of the skin. As we age, the skin becomes less robust and takes on a dry, wrinkly, leathery, and/or crepe paper-y quality. There are plenty of over-the-counter cosmeceuticals out there that you can use that smell nice and feel good on your face, but they don't do much to correct the long-term problem. This is why medical-grade skin care is useful, because it has that deeper penetration and can affect more long-term results.

I know, I know—as guys we have a hard time just remembering to wash our faces some days, let alone go through a six- to twelve-step skin care regimen every morning.

> **I TEND TO CUSTOMIZE OUR SKIN CARE REGIMEN FOR THE MALE AUDIENCE, BREAKING IT DOWN TO ONE OR TWO STEPS AT FIRST AND ENCOURAGING GUYS TO GET USED TO IT.**

Because of this, I tend to customize our skin care regimen for the male audience, breaking it down to one or two steps at first and encouraging guys to get used to it.

I had to do the same process for myself, starting out with a facial wash instead of just using Dial soap on my face. Once I got comfortable with that, I started introducing more, washing my face in the shower and then just rubbing the sunscreen on afterward. Eventually, I was able to move up to a third step, which was putting a skin treatment on my skin before the sunscreen, but that's about where I've stopped. Eventually I might be able to move up to a fourth step, but it's hard to get on that train.

Over the following pages, we'll cover a few of the skin care products that all guys should be using to protect their skin from the sun and to keep that virile, vital, youthful appearance strong.

SUN PROTECTION PRODUCTS

Ultraviolet (UV) radiation from the sun is the enemy of your skin. It causes wrinkles, spots, dryness, and skin cancer, and during healing from surgery it prevents scars from fading well. The ultraviolet light in sunlight is in two forms: ultraviolet A (UVA) and ultraviolet B (UVB). UVA rays age your skin by breaking down the supporting fibers. UVB rays cause skin cancer. Think UV(A) for Aging and UV(B) for Bad (skin cancer). You should avoid both, but it is especially important to avoid the UVB light—it is more dangerous.

Sunscreens fall into two basic categories: sunscreens and sunblocks.

Sunscreens are lotions containing chemicals such as avobenzone and oxybenzone to filter out the UV rays. They are effective, especially the ones with high sun protection factors (SPF), but they wash or sweat off easily and are not as good at blocking UVB light as the sunblocks are. Typically they are better at blocking UVA rays.

Sunblocks are basically the same as the thick white ointments you used to see lifeguards using on their noses. They contain minerals, usually zinc oxide or titanium, to physically block both UVA and UVB rays. In the newer formulations, the zinc or titanium is micronized, so the particles are very small and not visible. The sunblocks tend to feel thicker and a little cake-like; they can occasionally plug up your pores and lead to acne. However, they are unlikely to be absorbed into your body.

A word here about protecting all the parts of your body while out in the sun: you want to make sure that you're covering not just your face but your chest, neck, and the backs of the hands, as well. After the face, these are the most telltale areas to show sun damage and aging, but they are often neglected. When you're driving, for example, the backs of your hands are very exposed to UV light, even if it's cloudy outside. If you can, wear sunglasses and a hat, and something to protect the back of your neck, but don't feel like you have to go to extremes in covering yourself up. Some sun exposure on bare skin is beneficial in that it helps your body produce vitamin D.

HYDRAFACIAL

Another skin-improvement procedure that doesn't involve surgery or needles is the hydrafacial, a vortex-infusion technology that pushes fluid into the skin to increase buoyancy and its youthful appearance. In a way, the process works a lot like a steam cleaning: at the same time the process is pushing fluid into the skin, it's suctioning off the excess fluid, which is loaded with all the impurities that were clogging your pores. At the end of a hydrafacial session, we'll often show our patients the fluid collection container so that they can see all the grime that was covering their face without them knowing it.

The best part about this process is that there's zero downtime after use. You may have a little redness to your face for an hour or two afterward, but it goes a long way toward increasing your face's buoyancy and hydration. In fact, we see a lot of celebrities that do a hydrafacial before hitting the red carpet or attending big events. Groomsmen parties, too, will come in for a session about a week or even a few days before the wedding just to get cleaned up and looking their best.

HYDRAFACIAL TREATMENT

The whole process only takes about twenty minutes to half an hour, and the effects last from a month to six weeks. Depending on the grime level of the face, some guys may need weekly treatments at first to get them up to par, and then they can space out the treatments after that.

MICRO-NEEDLING

Before jumping into injections such as Botox and fillers, micro-needling is another way that we can encourage natural collagen production. The process is fairly simple, using a wand with a tip the size of a marker that's filled with about twelve to fifteen micro-needles that oscillate against the skin, encouraging the body to turn over old collagen and build those areas back up. This procedure is excellent for fine lines and wrinkles, and we often use it around the eyes, in the crow's feet area. We also use it around the mouth and neck, but it can also be done on the full face and neck.

MICRO-NEEDLING PROCEDURE

Before we start the procedure, we'll numb the area with numbing cream so that most of the time all you feel is the vibration of the wand against the skin. I've even had people fall asleep while the procedure was being done. To me, it felt like getting a close shave, no big deal. Afterward, you may have some redness in the skin that lasts for a day or two, but nothing more severe looking than a sunburn.

As with the hydrafacial, we recommend doing the micro-needling procedure in a series, coming in every six weeks or so to allow the new collagen to build up on itself.

BOTOX AND OTHER NEUROTOXINS

Botox is the more popular formulation of this toxin, but there are other drugs (Dysport and Xeomin) that work just as well. For ease of use, I'll use the word "Botox" to mean any of these three drugs. (It's a bit like using the term "Kleenex" for tissues.) Botox is a toxin that temporarily paralyzes the muscles that form lines and keeps them from contracting. With less contraction, the skin relaxes, the wrinkles soften, and the lines tend to fill in a bit on their own.

Men's use of Botox has increased dramatically in recent years, with Botox injections for men accounting for nearly 10 percent of all injectables procedures in 2016.[15] Men's use of Dysport and Xeomin has grown along with Botox, achieving a 337 percent increase between 2000 and 2014,[16] leading not only to an exponential growth curve for the procedure among men over the past four or five years, but also to a number of new nicknames, including Brotox, Protox (for professionals), and Scrotox (for more of the background on this one, check out chapter 17).

When it comes to application, men tend to need a stronger dose than women, mainly because we have bigger muscles and stronger facial features. The dose tends to last about three to six months, and the strength of the injection can range from

---

15   "Cosmetic Surgery National Data Bank Statistics 2016," American Society for Aesthetic Plastic Surgery, accessed April 10, 2017, http://www.surgery.org/sites/default/files/ASAPS-Stats2016.pdf.

16   Taylor, Peter Lane, "Brotox: It's Time for Men to Come Out of the Closet," *Forbes*, May 31, 2016, https://www.forbes.com/sites/petertaylor/2016/05/31/three-reasons-why-botox-will-change-every-mans-job-and-online-dating-prospects/#10d059ec2eb0.

partial to total paralysis. Personally, I tend to favor partial paralysis, as it allows for some movement; I'm not a fan of the skating rink forehead or the frozen bowling ball look. We still want to have some animation when we talk.

Popular areas for toxin injections in men include the glabellar area, which is the spot right between the eyebrows where the classic "11" lines form, as well as the forehead and around the crow's feet area of the eyes. Some people will also get Botox injections for a gummy smile or for the lower aspects of the jaw, or for more off-the-face procedures such as sweat reduction and the treatment of migraine headaches, which we get into more in the chapter on Fringe Procedures (see chapter 19).

BOTOX PROCEDURE

Essentially, what we're doing with the neurotoxin injections is softening the activity of those muscle attachments below the skin.

These muscle attachments are designed to pull down in order to achieve facial expressions, and the more they're pulled down, the more likely the skin is to form a wrinkle or furrow along the pull lines. What the neurotoxin injection does is halt that "pulling down" at the beginning of the process, stopping the muscle usage so that those connections aren't tugged down and the wrinkle isn't as prominent, allowing the skin some time to repair some of that longstanding damage.

With forehead injections, we'll often start at the top and correct some of the horizontal wrinkles of the forehead, then move down to the glabella, being careful to add enough to reduce the wrinkle but not so much that it completely paralyzes the area. Since men tend to need stronger doses of neurotoxin, we'll probably do between twenty-five and fifty units of Botox between the eyebrows and about sixteen to twenty units along the forehead, injecting the solution with incredibly fine needles similar in size to the kind diabetics use to prick their fingers four times a day.

Despite this, we still have some guys who get a little antsy when we come at them with a needle. These guys may have three gunshot wounds, a knife scar, and a tattoo but still go bananas when we tell them we're going to use a needle. In those cases, we'll offer some numbing cream before doing the injections.

Botox injections tend to last about four months on average, and there's zero recovery time after a procedure. In fact, some clients will come in during their lunch break or before they go into work for the day. The effects take about a week to kick in, gradually setting in until clients start to notice that they can't flex the injected muscles as strongly as they used to, or they can't furrow their brow as aggressively. When it starts to fade off, too, the effect is just as gradual.

PRECAUTIONS WITH NEUROTOXINS

There's a twofold precaution that people should be aware of when considering Botox: the first part is that if a neurotoxin is injected improperly and strikes an artery that feeds into the eye, it can cause permanent blindness. The second aspect of that precaution, then, is self-explanatory—don't allow anyone who isn't board certified to do a Botox injection on you. Only board-certified plastic surgeons, dermatologists, oculoplastic surgeons, and facial plastic surgeons, or those who are overseen by them, should do this procedure, as they're the only ones who truly understand the deep anatomy of the skin. An aesthetician or physician's assistant may not have this knowledge, and certainly not some hair dresser or day spa employee. Neurotoxin injections are a medical procedure, not a spa treatment, so be certain you're seeing a professional when you have this procedure done.

FILLER

As with Botox, the technology for fillers has drastically changed in recent years. In fact, it's become so effective that it's altered our practice's facelift rate, allowing us to get much more done and with less involvement, as well as avoiding the risks to the facial nerve and to the patient's sideburns and beard-wearing capability.

"Filler" is the common term for hyaluronic acid, a naturally occurring, water-loving substance that has been developed in such a way that it can take on a bevy of different forms, varying in consistency based on thickness, hydrophilic qualities, buoyancy, and even stretchability.

Before fillers became so refined, plastic surgeons would initially just attack a certain wrinkle and try to fill it in, almost like Spackle. Now that we've gotten back to the anatomy of the process including fat pockets, we can be more sophisticated in our approach to facial rejuvenation. Using the "Egg of Youth-fulness" analogy, we've found that adding the right consistency of fillers in the right locations can help augment, redefine, and rebuild a wide variety of facial features.

For example, one type of filler can be used around the temple to fill in that "sunken" look that comes with aging, while another type can be used around the eye orbit to fill in the lid/cheek junction from the lower lid to the upper cheek, where the bags under your eyes develop. Here the filler can be used to blend out some of the droopiness and augment the cheekbone, bringing that fat ratio back up and reversing the Egg of Youthfulness. Another plus of this particular filler is that, when used correctly, it avoids the appearance of having a little worm under the skin, the way older versions of fillers would appear under the eyes. Instead, the gel has been thinned and augmented with different components that allow it to fill in the area under the eye much more naturally.

Around the mouth and chin area, another filler can be used to blend out the nasolabial folds—those lines that extend from the corner of the nose to the corner of the mouth—softening them instead of removing them entirely in order to keep it natural looking. And around the mouth itself, yet another filler has been specially designed to work with the necessary elasticity of the mouth while filling in those sinking contours. This is especially beneficial to guys with those vertical smoker's lines around the mouth—the kind that, when you pucker up, result in deep, unattractive wrinkles.

There are other fillers that can specifically augment the lips, particularly the upper lip, where we lose a lot of fullness as we age and the area between the nose and the upper lip becomes longer, thinner, and deflated. However, this procedure isn't requested as often with guys unless they've had full lips their whole lives, like John Travolta or Val Kilmer.

Filler can also help with chiseling out the jowls and lifting them up. Again, if we rebuild the foundation of the cheek, we can lift some of those jowls with filler and bring out a more refined, stronger jawline look. The chin crease, too, can be softened out if it's become too prominent over time.

FILLER PROCEDURE

The filler procedure is pretty straight-forward. We can do the whole process in-office, starting with numbing the areas to be addressed with numbing cream and/or injecting anesthesia for a nerve block, and then injecting the filler. The filler itself also has a numbing component built into it, which is an improvement that's only been seen in the last few years, so the more filler we use, the better it feels, because that area is becoming more and more numb.

Depending on the procedure and type of filler used, the effects of the procedure will last anywhere from six months to two years.

FAT TRANSFER FILLER

Then there's the *au naturel* filler—your own fat. There are plusses and minuses to using your own, self-made filler, but the process is fairly straightforward. Essentially, we liposuction some fat from around the belly, or the arms or thighs, and then either clean it or run it through a machine to extract the healthy fat, separating it from the liquid and blood and making it into a consistent thickness. In some cases we'll extract the fat with more liquid and inject it directly, depending on which technique is more appropriate at the time.

We usually use between four and eight ccs of fat per side, which is equivalent to about a teaspoon or teaspoon-and-a-half of fat. Even though that doesn't seem like a lot, it's about two to three times the amount of filler we would use, as fat has a tendency to reabsorb into the body. That tendency is one of the drawbacks of using your own fat as filler. Anywhere between 30 and 70 percent of the fat can reabsorb or disappear, so we tend to fill up the area a little more, going one and a half to two times beyond where we want it to eventually end up and then waiting to see how much it's going to reduce.

Apart from reabsorption, another potential issue is the natural lumpiness of fat. This isn't visible in most areas of the face, but it can be visible when injected just underneath the eyelids, where your skin is thinnest. We're seeing more work being done with nanofat, which is even thinner than the microfat we typically use as filler and which can be injected even more superficially in areas of thinner skin, including the more crepe paper-y skin of the neck folds and around the mouth.

On the other hand, the positive side of using your own fat as filler is that not only is it permanent once it settles into place, but the fat continues to act like where it came from. If you have tendency to gain weight around the stomach, for instance, and we use stomach fat as filler, then the area we filled is naturally going to stay fuller.

FACELIFTS

Plastic surgeons have improved on the facial rejuvenation process quite a lot in recent years. In the past, we would basically just take the skin and pull it back, because the belief was that everything on the face had just "dropped" and needed to be pulled back into place. However, now that we're looking at anatomy a little more closely, we've realized there are finer aspects—certain fat pockets throughout the face that need to be repositioned or augmented to keep the natural appearance. Remember from the beginning of the chapter about the Egg of Youthfulness.

It's with all of that in mind that plastic surgery has changed its stance somewhat on facelifts and facial rejuvenation. Instead of just yanking it all back, which can lead to a very unnatural appearance, we reposition different aspects back to their original positions using the strength layer, refilling fat compartments and repositioning the skin in order to turn the egg "youth side up."

FACELIFT RISKS

There are just over forty muscles in the face, with a strength layer between most of the superficial layer and the deep tissue that's called the SMAS, which stands for the superficial musculoaponeurotic system. Typically, we're working to elevate that SMAS strength layer, which serves as our focal point for lifting everything back up to that youthful egg appearance.

While there are several different approaches to this, from minimally invasive to "deep plane," where you begin with where the bone and muscle meet and elevate from there, one of the most important things that plastic surgeons look out for is avoiding injury to the facial nerve.

If you were to lay your hand on your face with the palm at your ear and your fingers spread out like a fan and your fingertips touching your eyebrow, nose and chin, this would give you a good idea of where the facial nerve lies. The nerve has several different trunks that go up to your eyebrows and eyes, to your cheek, down to your smile and your chin, on and on. And severing part of that nerve could result in partial facial paralysis, which is why it's incredibly important to look out for.

Another thing that plastic surgeons have to be careful about, especially with men, is the risk of postoperative bleeding. Men tend to have slightly larger blood vessels than women, as well as slightly higher blood pressure. Because of this, the risk of complications from bleeding after a facelift is higher in men than it is in women. If bleeding does occur under any of the flaps we elevate, the postoperative complications can be pretty

drastic. A collection of blood pooling underneath an elevated facial flap, for instance, can
compress the normal blood flow to the flap
and cause the skin to die, leaving an open
sore. Because of this, we're very regimented
about follow-up procedures to ensure that
this does not happen.

One other aspect that may be an advantage
or a disadvantage, depending on how you
look at it, is the potential impact on your
beard growth. This can be an advantage
in that men can grow out their sideburns a
little to hide any small potential scars. On the
other hand, the adjustment and pull of the
skin that comes with a facelift can alter your
normal beard pattern, putting it more pos-
teriorly and potentially lessening your ability
to have a full beard.

FACELIFT PROCEDURE

With men, we'll typically make the incision
around the hairline either right at the junction
between the face and the ear, or slightly in

front of the ear, and then extend that incision under the earlobe and around the back of the ear into the hairline and the back of the head. By making the incision there, the surgeon gains access to most of the face, the angle of the jaw, and all the way into the neck under the chin. The surgeon could alter a turkey neck at this point, elevate the jowls and mid-face, and basically redevelop and recreate the normal anatomical contours of the face. For guys, this procedure usually involves correcting the jowls and neck.

The resulting scars are often well hidden and can easily be covered up with sideburns, and we make sure to put the scar well within the sideburn area. We're also careful to hide the curve of the incision in a crease or other curved aspect behind the ears, as men tend to keep their hair shorter. We also reposition the earlobes back to normal, which can be a telltale sign of facelift surgery, and can reduce the size of the earlobes at the same time as larger earlobes are also a sign of aging.

CHAPTER 10

HAIR TODAY, GONE TOMORROW

No "Daddy Do-Over" book would be complete without a section on hair.

Styles have changed a lot over the years, but the propensity to cover up with a foreign object like a toupee has, thankfully, fallen to the wayside as technology has advanced, and hair transplantation is not only easier but comes out looking far more natural. We're past the days where you have to make up excuses to your grandkids, like my dad does when any of my kids ask what happened to his hair. Inevitably, he'll answer that he either grew out of it, or that he has plenty of hair, it's just "clear" colored.

As we pointed out earlier in the chapter on the male dilemma, chapter 2, men have it easier when it comes to aging. The salt-and-pepper look is distinguished, and a lot of women find it attractive. When it comes to hair, while many of us prefer to let it turn gray, we don't want it to turn loose. In fact, a study showed that while men with bald or closely shaved heads may appear more dominant, they were also considered to be older and less attractive when compared to pictures of these same men with a full head of hair.[17]

THINNING HAIR

There are a lot of products out there that can help with thinning hair these days, from Propecia-type drugs that stop the produc-

---

17   Drake Baer, "People are psychologically biased to see bald men as dominant leaders," *Business Insider*, February 13, 2015, http://www.businessinsider.com/bald-men-signals-dominance-2015-2.

tion of dihydrotestosterone (DHT), which can cause hair loss, to drugs like Rogaine that can augment thinning hair. A recent advancement in PRP, platelet rich plasma, has also shown promise. Blood is drawn, then spun down in a centrifuge to separate the plasma, and then injected under the thin hairs to improve the thickness. Even these products, however, may not be entirely effective against genetics. In the end, all you need to do is look to your mother's father to find out how your own hair is going to turn up (or out).

HAIR TRANSPLANTATION

In the past, hair transplantation was about as artistic as putting up drywall. Surgeons would often just take a giant strip from the back of your head, extract as many follicles as they could, and then plug them back in where it was thinning on top. In fact, that was what they called them: plugs. And they looked just like plugs, too, in the same way that doll hair appears plugged—just naked skin for about half an inch, then a plug of hair, then bare skin again. It was unnatural appearing and very artificial.

Today, technology allows us to transplant hair much more seamlessly. Instead of taking a big strip from the back of the head and leaving a big scar there, surgeons can isolate small groups of three to five hair shafts, called a follicular unit, harvest it with an incision the size of a pin point, and move it to its new location. The units are grouped together more closely as well, and are varied so that you have some small units, some medium-sized ones, and some large ones.

> **TODAY, TECHNOLOGY ALLOWS US TO TRANSPLANT HAIR MUCH MORE SEAMLESSLY.**

After the procedure, there's a lag time where the initial transplants take hold and then fall out, followed by a waiting period of about two to three months as the new follicles grow in. A lot of guys get frustrated during this period, which is why we have to remind them that this is all part of the hair's life cycle. As the new units take hold, they'll put down their roots and grow out naturally from that point on. This "new" hair also tends to be more robust, as it comes from the back of the head, where the hairs are naturally stronger, often resulting in fuller, thicker coverage.

The most important aspect of this procedure is timing. You don't want to do a hair transplant too early in life, because there's always a chance you could lose more hair. It would look odd if you had a nice line of hair up front and then bare scalp until you reached the back of the head—like Friar Tuck, or some kind of strange clown.

HAIR TRANSPLANTATION PROCEDURE

The harvest and transplantation process is typically done under a local anesthetic using specialized instrumentation that works like a vacuum to suck up the incised follicular units. A technician separates the units out and then places them millimeters apart in the new implantation sites. It's a lot like planting, except in this case we're planting a field of hair across the top of your head instead of rows of corn.

Some surgeons will extract a large amount of hair at once and place it, while others will go back and forth between the back of the head and the new placement site. Either way, the entire procedure typically runs about two hours, with follow-up procedures scheduled if necessary.

BEARD AND MUSTACHE AUGMENTATION/ TRANSPLANTATION

Although not as popular a procedure in the United States, beard and mustache transplantation has been catching on overseas, particularly in the Middle East where full beards tend to be seen as symbols of masculinity. Guys who have more of a baby face or who have a hard time growing in a full beard because of patchy growth patterns or facial trauma earlier in life can also benefit from beard transplantation, though one has to be careful about the location from which they extract the new hair. Pubic hair is one alternative, though the placement can be tricky because of the orientation of the individual hair follicles (and really, who wants that on their face?). More often, the hair is removed from lower on the neck where the beard is often shaved off anyway, and transplanted to the desired area.

LASER HAIR REMOVAL

Back in college we used to joke with some of the guys to "take the sweater off" before a shirts and skins game, or when we hit the pool. They were just hairy beyond belief.

When it comes to hair removal, guys tend to want it removed from their chest, or from the upper back or the "butt-stache"—above the butt/lower back area. To do this, we often use a laser procedure, which targets the hair follicles and removes them in pulses.

The downside of this is that the lasers tend to only target darker hairs, so lighter blonde hair or gray hair, or even light brown hair, is often missed. The procedure is also difficult to use on darker-skinned individuals, as the laser has a harder time picking out the hairs against the contrast of the skin. Even olive-complexioned individuals may have a difficult time with the procedure.

Additionally, the permanent reduction in hair may only be about 30 percent of the total, which isn't quite the "permanent" we really want, so it can be frustrating for a lot of guys. Still, some guys will get the procedure done just before summer and take care of the remaining hair on their own, and if it helps with a furry sweater of a chest, even that 30 percent may make a big difference.

CHAPTER 11

EYES

Apart from owning and running his own insurance consulting company, my dad is also a pretty avid golfer and serves on the board of his local golf club. One day, my step-mom happened to attend one of the meetings, and afterward she asked him if anyone else cared that he slept through the whole meeting.

"I wasn't asleep—I was looking down and taking notes!" my dad said, but she swore it looked like his eyes were shut the entire time.

The problem is that my dad has heavy eyelids, which make it look like he's asleep most of the time—a condition that affects a lot of men, particularly as they age. The curve around the edge of the lid begins to turn down, and the entire face takes on a sad, tired, depressed look. No one wants to go through life looking like the cartoon character Droopy the Dog, which is why we often suggest any one of a number of eye surgeries, depending on what's needed to bring the eyes back to an open, more youthful appearance.

DO YOU REALLY NEED AN EYELID LIFT?

Maybe not. You might just need to get more sleep (I know, as a father of four, that is much easier said than done). You might also have seasonal allergies that are giving you bags under your eyes. And sometimes it's not the eyes that are the problem—it's the "11s," those two vertical lines between your eyes, also known as frown lines or glabellar lines. They can give your eyes a tired appearance and can also make you look stern and unapproachable.

The appearance of frown lines can be quickly improved with injections of botulinum toxin. Botox, the more popular formulation of this toxin—among the equally effective Dysport and Xeomin—temporarily paralyzes the muscles that form frown lines and keeps them from contracting. (As mentioned before, I'll use "Botox" to refer to any of these three drugs for simplicity's sake.) To relax frown lines, I will inject the Botox into five separate points between and over your eyebrows, using a fine needle that doesn't really hurt. Botox can typically be used between the eyes, on the forehead, and around the sides of the eyes (crow's feet). Occasionally, it can also be used for "smoker's lines" around the lips as well.

Filler, too, is an option, particularly with the lower lids, as it can be used to blend out the lid/cheek junction that's causing visible drooping or that dark, under-eye herniation. It's a tougher area to fill, as the skin is incredibly thin, but the moldability of filler makes it easier to smooth out. However, the downside of using filler for the lower lid is that it has to be manipulated manually to fill out the area properly, so it's often a fine balance of injection and physical manipulation to get the filler in without having to press against the eyeball to adjust it.

Like the Botox, filler is only a temporary fix, lasting from about six months to a year. However, it's a good option for people looking to avoid surgery. Laser surgery, too, can be performed, though it's not a procedure that I prefer to perform, as there can be some ripple effect from the heat of the laser on the surrounding skin. Call me a perfectionist, but I prefer the precision of the knife to a heat beam.

If you prefer a more permanent fix, consider doing an eyebrow lift before looking into eyelid lift surgery. More often, it's the eyebrow that needs to be adjusted before the eyelids. Think of it like a set of curtains, with the brow as the curtain rod and the eyelids underneath it as the curtain. If the rod is low, for example, the curtain can bunch up and fold into itself much more readily than if the eyebrow (the curtain rod) is in a normal, higher position. However, if you just trim the curtains, the eyebrows can continue to move downward on the face and reform the folds, at which point, if you decide to move the eyebrows up, you won't have enough curtain to cover the eyeballs.

Often we'll do both procedures together, both the brow lift and the eyelid lift, or we'll separate them out, starting with the eyebrow and then the eyelid.

Starting from the top, the first thing we do is ensure that the eyebrows maintain their straight across look, which is the more masculine-appearing position for the eyebrows. We don't want to have a big, elevated eyelid or eyebrow—the result would either make you look too feminine or like you just had six shots of espresso and are working on the seventh. And we don't want to make you look sad, with your eyebrows peaked in the middle and dropped on the outside.

SURPRISED   **ANGRY**   **NORMAL MALE**

There are three different types of brow lifts that we perform:

→ Endoscopic brow lift

→ Coronal brow lift

→ Direct excision brow lift

ENDOSCOPIC BROW LIFT

This is the most common brow lift procedure for both men and women, and involves the use of small cameras that are inserted through minor incisions along the hairline—one along the midline, another behind the hairline on each side at the lateral aspect of the orbital rim (outer edge of the eye socket).

The camera, which is placed at the end of a straight-line rod, is accompanied by small instrumentation that allows us to release the attachments of the eyebrow to the orbital rim. From there, we selectively take out several of the muscles at the glabella—the midline between the eyes at the top of the nose—reducing that downward pulling force but keeping some muscles in place so that your face still has animation.

After we've reduced those muscle fibers, we'll go in and elevate the eyebrows to an appropriate position, securing them in place with absorbable tacks or pegs, which dissolve over a period of several months. Anatomically, the downward force between the eyes and the top of the nose is negated, and the upward, elevating force of the forehead muscle takes over, keeping the brow elevated where it needs to be.

ENDOSCOPIC BROW LIFT RECOVERY TIME

This procedure can take about a week to ten days to recover from, and while swelling occurs, it's often not severe. Usually I'll leave a drain in place just to help the skin and muscle as it heals; occasionally we'll put you in a headband-type dressing for a few days as the incisions heal.

As with any surgical procedure, there's a risk of nerve damage, which would lead to numbness in your scalp, but this is reduced thanks to the use of the magnifying endoscopic camera, which helps us keep a much better eye on what we're doing and what attachments we're dividing.

CORONAL BROW LIFT

This procedure is a little more involved than the endoscopic and requires a long incision along the hairline—cut in a zigzag pattern so it doesn't look like you're wearing a headband—before folding the skin forward down to the orbital rim.

It sounds rough, but fortunately you don't have to see it. From here, we'll do the same detaching of the muscles that we'd do with an endoscopic brow lift and elevate things up. However, the big advantage of this process and where it varies from the endoscopic procedure is that we can also remove some of the protruding skin and potentially bring the hairline forward a bit, resulting in a smaller, more youthful forehead and a more uniform pull across it.

On the other hand, the disadvantage of this procedure is that you'll develop a numbness in your forehead and sometimes even back into your posterior scalp, as those divided nerves typically run from your eye socket to the back of your head, making it feel weird when you comb your hair. Additionally, there's the chance that you'll have a more visible scar right along the hairline.

Because of the chance of visible scarring, we tend not to do this procedure as often on men, and as endoscopic technology improves we're doing this procedure less overall.

CORONAL BROW LIFT RECOVERY TIME

Recovery from a coronal brow lift is at least two to three weeks, if not longer. There's also a lot more swelling involved than in other brow lift procedures, as well as a high risk of necrosis, or skin death, as you're dividing up some of the major blood vessels to that area. For these reasons, we hesitate to recommend this procedure if the endoscopic brow lift will suffice.

DIRECT EXCISION BROW LIFT

As the name suggests, this procedure is very direct. Basically, an eyebrow-type incision pattern is made directly above the current eyebrow that's at least the length of the eyebrow and probably about as wide. From there, we just elevate the eyebrow up, taking the skin out directly above it and tacking it into its new position.

This procedure is typically more applicable to older men. Though it used to be applicable to men in general, the tolerance for having a scar over each eyebrow has gone down tremendously since male plastic surgery has become more popular.

During this procedure you can also go after the muscles that you'd normally hit during an endoscopic brow lift, softening the glabellar area and forehead attachments.

DIRECT EXCISION BROW LIFT RECOVER TIME

Recovery on this procedure is pretty quick—usually about a week, if that. There's not much swelling, as you're not doing much dissecting to get from the back of the scalp to the eyebrows like you do with an endo-scopic procedure—you're already there. It's just a matter of letting that scar heal up and making sure the incision line is as close to the brow line as possible to be partly hidden. In this case, as with all brow lift procedures, it's important to use plenty of sunscreen from here on out to reduce the visibility of the scar line.

EYELID LIFT SURGERY

Eyelid surgery is very helpful in removing loose and sagging skin on the upper eyelid and loose skin and wrinkles on the lower eyelid. It's also great for reducing puffiness in the eyelids, by removing the bulging fatty stores. The surgery also removes bags from under the eyes and restores the natural skin color there. In general, I aim to restore the natural contours of your eyes and give them a more rested and youthful appearance.

I cannot, however, change the basic shape and structure of your eyes and the area around them. As with all plastic surgery, it's important to have realistic goals and expectations.

EYELID LIFT READINESS QUIZ

☐ **Has getting more sleep improved the appearance of your eyes?** If not, or if the improvement isn't enough, a lift might be needed.

☐ **Do you have seasonal allergies that cause watery eyes, bags under the eyes, and other visible changes around your eyes?** If your eyes look better when it's not allergy season, talk to your doctor about antihistamines. If your eyes still look unattractive when allergy season is over, think about an eyelid lift.

☐ **Do you drink alcohol often?** You might have baggy eyes the next morning. Cut back on alcohol to see if this makes a noticeable difference.

☐ **Are you prepared to spend a couple of weeks with swollen eyes after surgery?** Bruising and swelling might make you feel uncomfortable in a social setting for two to three weeks.

THE EYELID LIFT PROCEDURE

There has been a recent shift in our thinking in regard to aging around the orbit and eye area. When we look at the younger generation, what makes their eyes appear more youthful is actually not an absence of extra skin, but an apparent fullness around the eye itself. So, often, instead of removing the bulging fat from under the eyes, many surgeons prefer to reposition and/or add additional fat to the area in order to "fill up" this deflation. In the past, we "attacked" the fat bulges, which caused some patients to look older/and or cadaveric because too much fat was removed. A newer technique involves fat transfer that sometimes can avoid incisional surgery altogether in these areas.

Eyelid lifts, also called blepharoplasty, are typically done under general or local anesthesia or intravenous sedation. The surgery is very safe. If we do upper and lower lids only, the surgery takes about two hours. If we do a combo with the brow lift, it takes thirty to sixty minutes longer. Either way, you go home the same day. The recovery time is fairly short; any pain can be easily managed with mild medication.

To correct problems with the upper eyelid, I make an incision that runs along the natural crease of the eyelid. I use that space to remove fat pockets and excess skin and to tighten up the muscles. Because the incision is hidden in the crease and closed with very tiny sutures, the scar from it is basically invisible.

For the lower eyelid, I make an incision just below the lower lash line, where I can remove excess fat and skin and tighten up the muscles in the lower lid and in the bags underneath. Often I will release a ligament at the lid/cheek junction that is accentuating the appearance of the bags and smooth out this transition zone. I sometimes use a transconjunctival incision, which is made into the inner part of the bottom eyelid.

The under-lash incision is closed with the same sutures; the scar quickly fades away to become nearly invisible.

AFTER THE SURGERY

You will be in recovery for a short time, during which I will remind you of possible complications. A small amount of swelling and bruising is normal. But if there is a lot of swelling or pain in one eye or any sort of change in your vision, it could mean the rare result of bleeding into the eye socket, which could cause optic nerve compression. There are not many emergencies in plastic surgery, but this is one of them. Call me at once.

Though eyelid lifts are very safe, you may experience some slight bleeding just after the surgery. The risk of infection or other problems is very low; I will give you some antibiotic ointment to apply to the incisions twice a day for a few days. Pain from this procedure is usually not very severe and can be easily handled with mild painkillers.

Just after the surgery, your eyes will likely be pretty swollen and bruised and may remain so for the next few weeks. The best treatment for the swelling is a lot of ice packs to the eyes and keeping your blood pressure in the low to normal range. This is especially important during the first few days. Some patients have trouble closing their eyes at first; this is normal and changes quickly. As a precaution, I will prescribe ointment and drops to protect your eyes from getting too dry. The worst swelling will go down within a week to ten days. Once that happens, you can pretty much resume your normal activities—but no heavy lifting, please.

Until the swelling goes down, you probably won't be able to appreciate your rejuvenated eyes. It will take several weeks of anticipation before you see the full benefits of the surgery.

For the next six months to one year, you should avoid exposing your incisions to direct sunlight. We want to protect the delicate skin of your eyelids as it heals. If you must be in the sun, wear full-coverage sunglasses and a hat with a brim. After that, plan to maintain lifelong sun protection practices. Too much sunlight will age the skin, bring back the wrinkles, and/or make the scar more prominent. For most patients, the good results of an eyelid lift will last somewhere between ten and twenty years. The aging process continues, however, and gravity and your genes will always win in the end.

> **FOR MOST PATIENTS, THE GOOD RESULTS OF AN EYELID LIFT WILL LAST SOMEWHERE BETWEEN TEN AND TWENTY YEARS.**

CHAPTER 12

NOSE

One of the earliest uses of plastic surgery involved the nose. Although reconstruction of noses was mentioned as early as 3000 BC in ancient Egyptian texts, the most well-known historical plastic surgery to the nose was pioneered by Ayurvedic physician Sushruta in 800 BC. Back then, when various appendages were being chopped off as a

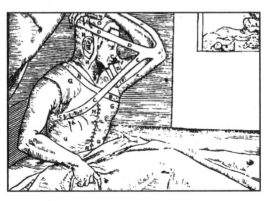

form of punishment, Sushruta developed a nasal reconstruction procedure that's still used today, taking skin cut from—but still attached to—the cheek, turning it, and using it to cover the area where the nose used to be.

Something that plastic surgeons generally have to stay aware of when it comes to noses is that guys tend to associate the size of the nose with the size of one's manhood. So, we have to be careful when doing any procedure around them.

For instance, when I was in plastic surgical training in Mississippi, I had a patient from the VA who didn't need much done, just a few skin cancers taken off of his nose, but the effect on him was awful. He went from being this rough and tough veteran to this emasculated mouse, just because the size of his nose was slightly reduced.

Apart from the perception of what the nose symbolizes, plastic surgeons have a lot on their hands when it comes to nasal surgery. The anatomy of the nose is surprisingly variable and very complex, so a little bit of change can go a long away.

NASAL COMPLEXITY AND HERITAGE PRESERVATION

First, when it comes to male noses, the skin tends to be thicker than it is with women, so we often need to make more significant changes underneath the skin to affect the external appearance. That's where rhinoplasty (nasal surgery) almost becomes like camouflage—there's a lot you can do under the hood to make the roof of the car look better, so to speak. For instance, we can take out a lot of the humps and bulges and any overriding length. We can also remodel some of the cartilage of the bone and improve the overall appearance.

Ultimately, the first time through on a nose job is going to have the best results, because the more work you do on the nose, the more problems you run into with support, scarring, and healing. You could end up with a situation where the nose basically collapses or it becomes so slender that it takes on a feminine appearance.

In general, men's noses are wider, thicker, and a little more angular and longer than women's. Think of the typical "masculine" nose—the Roman nose that sits on the face like a tipped over "L," jutting straight out and then down—compared to the typical slender "ski jump" of a woman's button nose, with that touch of an upturn at the tip. There's a clear visual difference between the two.

Of course, ethnicity plays a strong role in nasal surgery, as well. We need to keep in mind the hereditary qualities of a patient's nose that they may or may not want to keep. Any time I see a guy in the office for his nose, I ask if there's any aspect of his hereditary makeup that he wants to maintain in his final results—any homage to his descent that he wants to preserve. Sometimes they do and sometimes they don't. For instance, I had a client of Arabic decent come in to have a hump removed from his nose, which he felt was too indicative of his heritage. He explained that he was tired of the stigma associated with it and just wanted to "be American" and not be seen as one way or the other. Other patients, however, are entirely the opposite and want to preserve the visual reminders of their heritage as much as possible.

All of these factors make working on noses a fairly complex procedure. And that doesn't even include the fact that noses take a fairly long time to heal—often upward of a year.

DO YOU NEED A NOSE JOB?

Before going into the details of nasal surgery, I always ask my patients, "Are you comfortable with looking like a cartoon character for up to a year?"

I'll usually put it a little more gently than that, but the fact is that while your nose is healing, you may have a thickness, almost like a bulb, on the tip of your nose that will look abnormal for about a year. I had one patient describe it as looking almost like the ball nose of a clown. But that's the short-term reality of nose surgery, and patients should understand what they're getting themselves into.

Apart from explaining the healing process, I'll also ask patients if they're considering a nose job for functional or more aesthetic purposes. If it's functional, I'll dive a little deeper. For instance, are they considering a nose job because of breathing issues? If so, then we always ask that they do a trial run of antihistamines first, just to make sure the breathing issue isn't solely due to allergies.

Sometimes the reason they're considering a nose job is both functional and aesthetic, such as to repair a broken nose. We've seen a lot of guys who got in fights growing up and broke their nose three or four times, and now their wives are demanding that they get it fixed, or they're just tired of dealing with the breathing problems associated with it.

With broken noses especially, the septum—the midline portion of the nose—can be kicked over to the side, or bent, so that one side is impinging on the other and causing an obstruction. This can be corrected with septoplasty, where the septum is straightened out and a portion may be removed.

Other nose conditions that we typically see guys for are naturally crooked noses, humps, or bulbous tips, all of which can be corrected with manipulation of the cartilage and the bone underneath the skin.

CHIN AND NOSE RELATIONSHIP

At the same time we're looking at the nose, we'll also assess the chin as the overall connotation of the masculine appearance is a broad, L-shaped nose and a strong chin. If the chin is recessed, that can have a huge impact on the guy's overall confidence level, both internally and the level of confidence he projects. If the chin-to-nose angle is too far back, we'll offer a chin implant or chin surgery to help augment the chin structure.

> **IF THE CHIN-TO-NOSE ANGLE IS TOO FAR BACK, WE'LL OFFER A CHIN IMPLANT OR CHIN SURGERY TO HELP AUGMENT THE CHIN STRUCTURE.**

Many times it's a matter of optical illusion—the nose may not be that big or long, but if the chin is recessed, it may seem that way. So, if we can bump the chin out a bit, then the nose will appear much more in line without having to undergo nose surgery.

NASAL SURGERY PROCEDURE

As I noted before, nasal surgeries can be incredibly complex, depending on what needs to be done. A humped nose, for instance, would require shaving down the bone at the top of the nose, followed by a repositioning of the bones so that they neatly tip back inward. With a bulbous nose, the focus is more on the lower cartilage, but reconstruction is still a careful and delicate process.

In most cases, I do an open rhinoplasty, which is where we make an incision at the base of the nose in the skin between the nostrils, and then lift everything up and do the dissection. From there we divide up several of the ligaments that are keeping the cartilage in place, including those that are keeping the cartilage at an improper angle, and reorient them appropriately. There are several things we can do at this point to manipulate the various nasal components to adjust the tip, height, projection, nostril width, and width of the nose itself, among other enhancements.

One of the most challenging parts of the process, however, doesn't come until after the surgery: keeping the nose completely immobile while it heals. The nose isn't like an arm or a leg—you can't throw it in a cast and keep it stable. Instead, all we can do is put a splint on the outside and some silicone splints on the inside, and even with those we only keep them in for about a week before they become too uncomfortable and too gunked up to be of use. Murphy's Law, too, states that something inevitably will happen to your nose almost as soon as we take the splint off. It could be as simple as walking behind someone and asking them a question, and they turn around in such a way that your nose smacks into their elbow or their hand. Or you slam the door on your nose, or your kid throws a toy at you and hits you squarely on the bridge. It's just something you have to be incredibly careful about, because you don't have that cast in place to keep your nose from getting knocked out of place.

The surgery takes about three to four hours, and patients usually go home the same day. You may have raccoon eyes like you just got punched in the nose (because we're breaking your nose on purpose), but those will fade quickly. In all, it takes about six to eight weeks for the bones to heal, and during that time we recommend that you avoid most activity, including weight lifting, running, and jogging as these can jar the bones. It is certainly advisable to avoid any aggressive activity or team sports.

CHAPTER 13

CHIN/NECK

Chin work can be a part of your nasal evaluation or procedure, since the two components are so strongly and visibly tied to each other, or it can be addressed separately. A strong chin is certainly a desired masculine trait, and while growing a beard or a goatee can enhance it, some guys want to ensure that their chin looks strong regardless of whether it's bearded or bare. Part of this may be due to what we talked about earlier in the section on the strong business exec look in chapter 3—"The size of the chin directly correlates to the level of the male sex hormone testosterone in the body. In other words, the larger the chin, the more testosterone, and thus a stronger sex drive."[18]

---

18   Jean Haner, "Signs of Sexuality in the Face," New Spirit Journal Online, April 11, 2015, http://newspiritjournalonline.com/signs-of-sexuality-in-the-face/.

Double chins can also be a big concern for guys, and it's a concern that's grown significantly since the advent of selfies and video calls. We've had dozens of dads and granddads come in who are just shocked at the amount of fat under their chin, or by their turkey neck, because they never noticed it until they started FaceTiming with their kids or grandkids.

Fortunately, a lot of these conditions can be corrected relatively easily.

LOVE YOUR SELFIE—DOUBLE-CHIN FAT REMOVER

The number one reason that most people have a heavy, or double, chin is due to extra fat. The area under the chin is one of the last places your body loses fat. In fact, we've seen guys come in who were in great shape, with six-pack abs and incredibly fit, but they still couldn't get rid of that pocket of fat under their chin.

> **THE AREA UNDER THE CHIN IS ONE OF THE LAST PLACES YOUR BODY LOSES FAT. IN FACT, WE'VE SEEN GUYS COME IN WHO WERE IN GREAT SHAPE, WITH SIX-PACK ABS AND INCREDIBLY FIT, BUT THEY STILL COULDN'T GET RID OF THAT POCKET OF FAT UNDER THEIR CHIN.**

One patient in particular had an entire family with this condition. His father had a double chin and so did his grandfather. All of them were healthy and stayed in shape, but when it comes to genetics there's not much you can do apart from surgical correction.

To correct a double chin, there are a few options:

➜ Liposuction

➜ Kybella injections

➜ Neck lift

➜ Direct excision of fat

We'll speak about liposuction in chapter 15, which is a good option if you're already having some face work done or you want to use that fat as a filler for your face or hands (see the section on filler in chapter 9).

As a less invasive procedure, Kybella is ideal for removing the superficial fat under the chin, fat that is close to the surface of the skin. Kybella is a series of injection treatments of deoxycholic acid, a naturally occurring biosalt that dissolves fat as permanently as liposuction. However, if the fat is deeper—that is, close to the floor of your mouth and behind the platysma muscle (the sheet of muscle that extends from your chest, over your collarbone, along the sides of the neck, and to the jawline)—then direct fat excision may be the best option, with or without Kybella.

KYBELLA

Kybella is typically done in a series of two to six treatments, consisting of shots similar in size to Botox.

We'll begin by mapping out the area on the chin where the injections will go, being sure to avoid nerves and taking a very specific and scientific approach to how the injections will be administered—instead of just eyeballing it and saying, "Okay, you have some fat here. Let me inject it."

Once the area is mapped, we'll do some numbing procedures, including icing the area and/or using numbing cream before beginning the injections. The injections themselves create a sensation of heat in the area, which some guys have compared to taking a shot of whiskey (and some have asked if they could have that whiskey before starting the shots). The entire process takes between twenty and thirty minutes, with ten minutes of numbing beforehand.

Noticeable swelling does take place after the injections are administered and can last for about two weeks, and there may be a numbness in the neck for about four to six weeks, but this is just a sign that the substance is working. It may make it harder to shave for a while, but we just remind our patients to be careful with the razor until the numbness fades. As the fat dissolves, the skin reacts and begins to retract back up, permanently creating a much more acute chin angle and overall a more fit, stronger appearance and more chiseled jawline.

NECK LIFT

When the fat below the neck gets to the point where it's bulging too much or the skin has drooped too much to retract following Kybella and/or liposuction treatment, a neck lift is your next best option.

This surgical procedure involves creating an incision around the outline of the ear underneath the earlobe, behind the ear and then to the back of the hairline, so that the neck skin can be elevated. Overall, the process is very similar to a facelift (for more on facelift procedures and recovery times, see chapter 9).

DIRECT EXCISION OF FAT WITH CORSET PLATYSMAPLASTY

Occasionally we can also do a direct excision of fat from the neck, starting with a horizontal incision at the base of the chin and dissecting down toward the Adam's apple. From here we can remove fat directly and manipulate the muscles to straighten them out and prevent any hanging of the platysma muscle. This procedure is also called a corset platysmaplasty and serves to create a tightening of that platysma muscle (like a woman's corset) that eliminates thick neck cords. However, it cannot remove loose, sagging skin.

TURKEY NECK

Speaking of loose, sagging skin, "turkey neck" is another chin condition that is best treated with a neck lift with or without corset platysmaplasty. This is because the condition isn't caused by fat nearly as much as it's caused by thin, loose skin.

More often than not, we'll treat the turkey neck with a neck lift as part of a facelift, because the incisions are made in similar areas. We can then elevate the facial skin along with pulling the excess skin up evenly and tightening it. In some cases, we might recommend a platysmaplasty instead, as this approach may work better for the tightening procedure.

NECK SURGERY RECOVERY

Recovery for any of the surgical neck procedures is about two to three weeks, during which time we are careful to avoid any fluid buildup that may put pressure on the skin.

Because of this, we always ask our neck surgery patients to avoid resting their chin on their hand, and instead adopt an "elbows on their knees" position when sitting. This position opens up the angle of the neck and avoids compression of the area, keeping the blood flow healthy and robust.

We also recommend that you lay down and sleep flat on your back for the first couple of weeks so that if there is any swelling, the fluid will go toward the back of your head as opposed to the neck area, where it can affect the blood flow. Also, the fluid can gather around your airway, creating a sub-jective feeling of choking in some patients.

NECK PROCEDURE PRECAUTION

One concern that I hear occasionally from patients undergoing neck procedures, usually only with Kybella, is that they sometimes develop the sensation that they can't breathe or swallow, or can't maintain their saliva.

I assure them that this is not the case with Kybella—this sensation is purely subjective, and neither your airway nor your esophagus is being compressed. If some swelling is occurring, or if a patient perceives swelling to be occurring, they may become anxious about this sensation and potential airway compression, but it's truly just a case of mind over matter. There is no mechanical obstruction, and the sensation should go away after a few days. If this occurs after neck lift surgery, the same is likely to be true, but it is always advisable to discuss it with your surgeon or seek medical assistance.

CHAPTER 14

CHEST

Gynecomastia. Guys may call it man breasts, man boobs, bitch tits, all kinds of things, each being just another way to describe male pattern breast tissue— an enlargement of the breasts that can be caused by anything from excessive weight gain to genetics to breast cancer.

Josh was a sixty-plus-year-old man who was dragged into my clinic by his wife because, for years, he wouldn't take his shirt off at the pool. Now he was embarrassed to even take his grandkids to the pool. His wife and, more importantly, he as well, were fed up with this and desired a change. He is not unlike many of my patients. He underwent a simple gynecomastia excision surgery and is happy to report he feels confident and even excited to get back to the pool and enjoy his grandkids. "How silly it was for me to feel ashamed, when the solution was so easy," "I should have done this years ago," and "I wish I didn't waste all that time hiding" were some of his comments to me afterwards.

It really is a common condition. According to research published in the *Cleveland Clinic Journal of Medicine*, gynecomastia "is present in 30 percent to 50 percent of healthy men."[19] It tends to develop earlier in life, often because of hormone imbalances between estrogen and testosterone, or through excess weight gain, the use of steroids, or even too much pot smoking. Other causes include testicular tumors or breast cancer. Side effects from the chronic use of certain medications can be found as a cause of gynecomastia as well.

19   Shirley A. Bembo, et al., "Gynecomastia: it's features and when and how to treat it," *Cleveland Clinic Journal of Medicine* 71 no.6 (June 2004): 511-517, http://www.mdedge.com/ccjm/article/94215 drug-therapy/gynecomastia-its-features-and-when-and-how-treat-it.

The most frequent cause of gynecomastia, however, is idiopathic: unknown origin. We don't have a known cause, and in a lot of those cases, the guy has just put up with it for a number of years and is now just tired of it.

Because the condition can occur in younger individuals, we often recommend waiting to do any kind of breast reduction surgery until the patient is past his last growth spurt, usually in his late teens or early twenties, to make sure he's not going to even out naturally first.

TYPES OF GYNECOMASTIA

There are three basic types of gynecomastia:

(1) Fibrous, where the mass appears like a giant marble underneath the nipple or in the breast. These are usually hard and stuck in place, so they need direct excision to be removed.

(2) Diffuse, where the tissue is more fatty and closer in appearance to a female breast, which is softer and more mobile. These can often be taken care of with liposuction.

(3) Fibrous-diffuse combination, where the hard, fibrous components are hidden deep in the diffuse fatty tissue, which often means that we'll need to do a combination of direct excision and liposuction to remove it.

GYNECOMASTIA EVALUATION GRADES I-IV

There are four levels of gynecomastia, ranging from grade I, which is minor enlargement with no real excess of skin, to grade IV, which is like a B or C cup on a woman.[20] With grade IV, the nipple is often displaced,

---

20   Wollina, U. and Goldman, A., "Minimally invasive esthetic procedures of the male breast," *Journal of Cosmetic Dermatology* 10 (2011): 150–155.

appearing lower on the pectoralis major muscle than is typical.

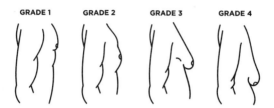

GRADE 1 GRADE 2 GRADE 3 GRADE 4

MALE BREAST PROCEDURE EVALUATION

Breast surgery is generally very safe, but not if you're a smoker. During the surgery, it is critical to maintain good blood flow to the nipple area. If you smoke, the nicotine causes the blood vessels in your body to contract—in your fingers, your toes, and your nipples. This is why I require patients who smoke to abstain from any kind of nicotine product—smoking, nicotine patch, e-cigarette, cigars, etc.—for six weeks before and after surgery.

I will also need to know if you have type 2 diabetes or high blood pressure. These conditions can also cause problems with blood flow and can slow down incision healing. If these issues have been addressed and are under control, I can safely operate.

BREAST REDUCTION PROCEDURES

LIPOSUCTION

If the tissue is mainly fatty and diffuse, or a fibrous-diffuse combination, we'll usually make a small incision about the width of your little finger on the lateral aspect (outer edge) of the breast, near the fold where the pectoralis major muscle ends. When it heals, the incision tends to blend in and just look like a little scratch on the side of your chest, where it falls into those normal contours.

DIRECT EXCISION

One guy, who was a workout fiend, came in to see us because he couldn't stand his "puffy" nipples. He did everything he could at the gym to build enough muscle to hide them, but they continued to just pooch forward. I explained that the condition wasn't anything he could exercise away—the condition was due to a fibrous component buried deep behind his nipple.

We did a direct excision to remove the mass, and the results were great. The puffiness was gone and the scar hid inconspicuously right along the nipple.

To do a direct excision, we'll make the cut right under the surface of the nipple, from about nine to three o'clock, then lift the nipple up like a top hat, coring out the fibrous tissue and then tacking the nipple back down. Occasionally we have to extend the scar like a smiley face, taking it horizontally a little more to the left or right if we need to, but most of the time I'm able

Above: Direct incision.

to work with the space I have and keep the scar within the confines of the nipple.

COMBINATION LIPOSUCTION AND DIRECT EXCISION

If we need to use both procedures, I'll usually start with the liposuction to remove as much of the diffuse tissue as possible, and then I'll go in and take out the fibrous components. With the liposuction, I'll also smooth out the contours of the outer edge of the breast, just to make sure it feathers out along the edge and doesn't create a shelf of remaining fat as it heals.

EXTENSIVE CHEST REDUCTION PROCESS

This complex surgery, used for grade III gynecomastia, involves removing excess skin, shaping chest tissue, tightening the remaining skin to achieve elevation of the NAC (nipple areolar complex), and maintaining blood flow to this area.

We may use liposuction if you choose to have some of the fat around the upper chest removed; it is not often performed for a full reduction. We can also reduce the fat in the "tail" of the chest tissue where it meets the underarm tissue and the back. In some cases, we can extend the under-chest incision to the back and do something similar to a gut tuck along the trapezius muscle below the scapula.

The reduction procedure takes about three hours, sometimes a little longer. Using liposuction takes additional time. Grade III gynecomastia can be a bit more challenging and take more time simply because the breasts are bigger to work with. Almost all of my patients spend just a couple of hours in recovery and go home the same day.

GRADE IV GYNECOMASTIA PROCEDURE

We treat grade IV gynecomastia much like we do a breast lift for women, except that with men, we're reducing the excess tissue and avoiding projection of the nipple. Instead, we want the muscle to be the projecting portion, so oftentimes we'll do a direct skin excision with nipple replacement or repositioning. This procedure involves what we call a free nipple graft, where we remove the nipple entirely, remove all the bulk behind it, and then pull the skin downward, placing the scar in the natural fold at the bottom portion of the pectoralis muscle before repositioning the nipple. This is also the type of chest procedure I'll perform for a person who is transitioning from the female to male gender. As a reminder, to locate a surgeon for other gender transitional changes, I encourage you to visit the ASPS at www.plasticsurgery.org.

This is a much more extensive surgery, and much riskier. The blood flow has to redevelop and reform underneath the nipple, so we'll do some specialized suturing to secure the nipple and make sure it doesn't move. If it's dislodged, then it will take longer to develop that blood flow. There's also a risk that the blood flow won't be reestablished at all, and the nipple could be partially or completely lost.

Grafting of the nipple can also have an impact on coloration. In darker skinned individuals, the nipple can change color, becoming pink or even white, either temporarily or permanently.

AFTER THE SURGERY

After the surgery, you can expect some numbness in the nipples. This will fade over time (but could take as long as six months). The greater the reduction, the more likely the numbness will last for a few months. Be patient, and give it time. Almost everyone regains sensation within a year. If you had grade IV reduction surgery with free nipple graft, you will have permanent numbness to your nipples. Fortunately, for most men this tends not to be noticed.

After the surgery, you will need to wear compression garments continuously for the first two weeks. After that, you can go to twelve hours a day for the next two weeks.

Because of the amount of tissue we remove in chest reduction, you may have some bruising in the area and some oozing from the incisions for the first few days. This is normal. Problems with wound healing and skin breakdown tend to be the most common complication. If you're overweight or have diabetes, the risk of wound-healing complications is much higher—upward of 50 percent of these patients will experience an opening in the wound. If you get one that opens up and oozes, we will treat it locally and give it time to heal from the inside out.

The pain after this procedure is generally quite manageable. We will prescribe some painkillers for the first few days. After that, you will likely be able to manage quite nicely without pain meds and switch to over-the-counter medication. Most patients are back to normal activities, except heavy lifting, within a week to ten days. The heavy lifting can be resumed around six weeks. You won't have any drains, and you will be able to shower after your second day at home. I will see you a week later to check on your healing. The scarring can be minimized by gentle massage and using a silicone scar cream.

During the healing, patients may sometimes develop masses in the chests. These masses are not cancer. They are typically fatty necrosis—nodules that form in the area under and around the nipples because the blood flow isn't as robust as before. These masses usually soften and heal up on their own, but sometimes this necrosis can persist for longer than a year and might need to be removed.

With my women patients, I require that chest reduction patients get baseline mammograms before the surgery so we can determine that there are no preexisting issues. This is not as important in men but will occasionally be required if family history warrants a concern. After the surgery, I ask you to check your chest area regularly. If you notice a lump, then you should consult with me before seeing any other doctor. I want to avoid you having a biopsy by a surgeon who doesn't realize that the blood flow has been altered. If a biopsy is recommended, we just have to be more thoughtful in performing this.

Your chest reduction should be trouble-free for many years. Fluctuations in weight can cause changes, so you should try to maintain a stable weight, but overall, the problems you experienced due to gynecomastia will be gone for good.

> **YOUR CHEST REDUCTION SHOULD BE TROUBLE-FREE FOR MANY YEARS. FLUCTUATIONS IN WEIGHT CAN CAUSE CHANGES, SO YOU SHOULD TRY TO MAINTAIN A STABLE WEIGHT, BUT OVERALL, THE PROBLEMS YOU EXPERIENCED DUE TO GYNECOMASTIA WILL BE GONE FOR GOOD.**

INSURANCE COVERAGE

It can be difficult to get insurance coverage for gynecomastia surgery, mainly because most insurance companies want the condition to be longstanding before they'll cover it. They want to see that you've done weight loss, and they'll make you jump through all the hoops, including one last one, which is proving that your gynecomastia is malignant—the equivalent of male breast cancer.

The catch is that the only way to determine that last condition is to take the whole thing out and let a pathologist look at it.

We can do needle biopsies and samples all day long, but the risk of that is what's called "sample bias." For example, say we look at a football-shaped mass, and we take a sample from where the laces would be. If the cancer is down toward one of the narrow endpoints, then we're going to miss it. In that case, the best way to determine if the tissue is malignant is to remove it entirely.

It's a circular issue with insurance, and it's all semantics. The same surgery is basically performed, so we usually end up just treating it as a cosmetic procedure. This is about a third of the cost that the procedure would be if it were treated as insurance "cancer-removal" surgery.

OTHER CHEST PROCEDURES

Apart from chest reduction, other chest procedures that men often consider are:

- ➜ Areola reduction
- ➜ Nipple reduction
- ➜ Nipple inversion correction

When you choose more than one procedure, I usually recommend that we do them at the same time. It's faster, easier, and less expensive to do the procedures at the same time. The time in surgery isn't usually much longer, and the recovery period is the same.

AREOLA REDUCTION

The areola is the circular, pigmented part of the chest surrounding the nipples. Over time, the areola may become darker, larger, and even look puffy. This in itself can be unattractive, but if you have gynecomastia surgery, the areola may seem disproportionately large afterward unless it is also reduced during the surgery.

The surgery itself is simple. I use a device that actually looks a lot like a cookie cutter to make a circular incision that is only skin deep all around the edge of the existing areola. Then I use a somewhat smaller cookie cutter to make another incision concentrically within the first. I will remove the skin in between and sew the new edges together with dissolving sutures to make an areola that's smaller and more symmetric. The whole procedure is very quick. If we do it combined with another surgery, it usually only takes about ten minutes per areola. If done as a stand-alone, it takes about thirty minutes per areola.

Nearly all the areola reductions I do are part of other chest work, and my patients generally don't experience any additional discomfort from the reduction. If you have only the areola reduction, the pain is minimal, and you can return to normal activities within a couple of days. The scarring is very minimal and fades to nearly invisible within a few months.

Most patients heal up quickly from this procedure and end up with symmetrically round areolas, although occasionally the areolas will stretch a bit and become more oblong or oval. These results depend on how much stretch is left in your skin, and how you heal.

You may have some pigmentation changes during healing; sometimes the area will look a bit splotchy, but that usually goes away on its own. Some patients experience loss of sensation in the area, but it almost always returns within six months. The improvement is permanent.

NIPPLE REDUCTION

Nipple reduction can be done as part of a larger procedure or on its own. As there are many different ways to perform this procedure, I will examine the condition and individualize the treatment plan to you and your specifics.

My goal is to keep the blood flow to the nipple. Sensation in the area is often reduced at first, but the numbness gradually goes away. If you should desire only a nipple reduction, it can be done as an office procedure under local anesthetic, and you can go home the same day. The pain of a nipple reduction alone is fairly minimal, and you can get back to your usual activities in just a couple of days. If there is any scarring at all (often there is none), it is very minimal.

INVERTED NIPPLES

I sometimes see patients with inverted nipples—the nipples are pulled inward instead of projecting outward. Because nipple inversion can be a sign of breast cancer, the first thing I ask is that you see a family doctor to rule out this possibility. Once you have the go-ahead, we can proceed to discuss the solution.

Normal nipples are everted—they stand out naturally from the areola. The nipple is held erect by a cylindrical column of muscle. When that muscle column is damaged or just not very strong, the nipple inverts.

To fix the problem, I use a tiny suture as a sort of hammock that I stitch into place under the nipple. It supports the base of the nipple so it everts outward and can't be retracted back in. Another approach is to take a little wedge of tissue from the base of the muscle cylinder and tuck that up underneath to provide a permanent support system.

Correcting inverted nipples is a fairly quick and simple procedure; it can be done under local anesthesia, generally takes only about thirty minutes, is not very painful, and leaves little to no scarring. You can generally resume normal activities within a day or two.

CHAPTER 15

BEER BELLY AND LOVE HANDLES

Weight gain can be a challenging problem for dads. As we get older and our metabolism rate decreases, it is often too late when we realize we just can't eat like we used to. I remember eating a large pizza pie each night during my freshman year at Notre Dame. Unfortunately, for this dad and many others, those days are over. I mentioned earlier how appearances can affect our performance in the boardroom. One part of our bodies is paramount in this situation: if our beer bellies are poking through our shirt, it is much more difficult for someone to take us seriously than if we are in shape, and our confidence dwindles as well.

But it's not just the workplace where this part of our appearance can be impactful. Being overweight can severely hinder our lives in the bedroom as well. Forget the time after you suffered through a chick flick with your wife and now realize she is comparing your flabby gut to the chiseled twenty-something star of the film. Ignore the hit that takes on your confidence, and consider this one instead: for every fifty pounds overweight you are, you lose an inch of length to your penis. In a recent study, a survey of a thousand British men revealed that about a third were not able to see their own penises when standing ... due to the size of their gut![21] So, dealing with excess weight in your abdominal region truly can be a case of improving life in the boardroom AND the bedroom.

21   Lindsay Abrams, "1 in 3 Men Can't See His Penis," *The Atlantic*, November 6, 2012, www.theatlantic.com/health/archive/2012/11/1-in-3-men-cant-see-his-penis/264615.

GUT TUCK

When the stomach has been stretched out with extra weight gain, the rectus abdominis muscles (your six-pack) can be permanently stretched out of place as well. They should face forward, but excessive weight gain can stretch out the tough band of fibrous tissue that runs down your midline (think of the row of buttons on a button-down shirt), causing the muscles to be shifted off to the side. When that band is stretched, it doesn't usually snap all the way back. (Think about when you stretch out the neck of an undershirt. Even after washing, it never really tightens back up.) The result is that beer belly you see when you turn sideways. Instead of your old flat gut, you look a little thicker from front to back. You can suck it in and try to hold it, or you can do crunches in the gym religiously every day, but you won't be able to tighten that fibrous connective tissue back down on your own.

Weight gain also stretches the skin of the abdominal area, often beyond the point of repair. Once you lose that weight, the skin appears saggy, wrinkled, and may have some stretch marks. The belly button is widened and may even be pointing south. Stretch marks may have appeared as your body expanded faster than your skin; the elastic fibers below the skin broke, causing reddish streaks. Dieting, exercise, and expensive creams alone can't return your skin to its original condition.

This is where you begin to consider the gut tuck (abdominoplasty, aka "tummy tuck"). This will give you a flatter, tighter abdomen, and if you have stretch marks it will remove most of those, as well. You might even choose to combine it with a bit of liposuction (discussed further later in the chapter).

GUT TUCK READINESS QUIZ: ARE YOU READY?

- ☐ Are you within 10 percent of your ideal body weight?

- ☐ What have you done to get back into shape?

- ☐ Have you had any other surgery on your abdomen?

- ☐ Are you looking to remove skin and fat from this area, or just decrease your overall bulk?

- ☐ Can you grab ahold in front of your abdominal muscles, or is your gut just pooched out without the external fat?

- ☐ Do you like your beer, just not your beer belly?

- ☐ Will you continue to eat well and exercise after the surgery? Weight gain will undo the surgical benefits.

The first thing to note is that a gut tuck is not weight loss surgery. In some cases, the gut tuck can be just the motivator you need to get serious about losing weight. A body that is closer to its previous normal as a result of exercise and a healthy diet is one that will benefit most (and heal and recover more quickly) from the surgery and experience the best results.

> **THE GUT TUCK CAN BE JUST THE MOTIVATOR YOU NEED TO GET SERIOUS ABOUT LOSING WEIGHT.**

THE GUT TUCK EVALUATION

We start with an office evaluation to assess your abdominal skin and fat, determine if there are any stretch marks or other scars on your abdomen, and feel along the midline to identify any widening that needs to be tightened. I will use the "pinch test" to see what can be removed. I will assess how you carry your fat and the degree of your skin's stretchiness to determine how it can move (and how much can be removed) during surgery.

As mentioned earlier, men tend to store most of their fat as visceral fat under their muscles, which makes the stomach feel solid when you push on it. The muscle is strong, and the fat is internal.

Everyone has *some* internal visceral fat. We can't remove that, but the plication (tightening) of the midline can help push that fat back into your body somewhat. When that happens, the overall thickness of your body from front to back is decreased. A side note here: the only way to reduce your visceral fat is to work it off with cardiovascular exercise and diet. Visceral fat is also associated with health problems, including type 2 diabetes and heart disease. Doing what you can to get rid of it is important.

I will evaluate your midline and see if there is any unremitting widening from previous weight gain. The fibrous band that runs down the center of your abdomen, when widened, is called a diastasis recti. This vertical bulge pushes out and makes you appear thicker and heavier from front to back.

Finally, we will assess your love handles. I will determine if you're a good candidate for combined liposuction (lipoabdominoplasty) in a single surgery or if liposuction should be performed at a later time in a separate surgery.

Once we've completed the full assessment, I can determine if a standard gut tuck is necessary or if a mini gut tuck might suffice. The main difference between the two has to do with the length of incision and whether or not we reposition your belly button. The mini procedure has a smaller incision but also has smaller results. Since the belly button (umbilicus) sits on a stalk and is tethered to the strength layer underneath your skin, we can only pull downward so far without releasing it. The mini gut tuck only cuts out a small ellipse of skin and fat below the belly button. The standard gut tuck can reposition the belly button and, therefore, remove significantly more skin and fat from the abdominal region in a football configuration. This is a decision we can make together with the information from your evaluation.

THE GUT TUCK SURGERY

The first step in the surgery is to release the belly button with an incision. Here, an incision is made around the visible surface of the belly button on the stomach and the umbilicus below it—a now-defunct tube that extends from your skin's surface deep through the fat—is dissected out to its base, where it awaits repositioning.

Next, an incision is made down to the muscle layer and extended out toward each hip bone. This exposes a football-shaped area of skin and fat to be removed. The dissection continues past the belly button, freeing enough tissue that it can be pulled down toward your toes, like a window shade. The rectus plication is performed next, by tightening the widened fibrous band, reorienting the six-pack muscles, and repositioning the now-smaller belly button. The previously stretched-out, wrinkly football of abdominal skin and fat is punted from your body, and the incisions are closed.

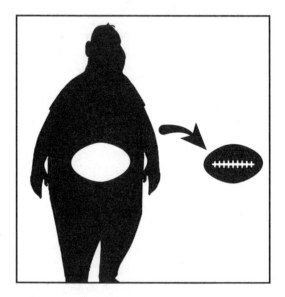

If you are also having liposuction, we do that before we close the incisions. This is a good time to do liposuction for those love handles, because we already have access; we can do better contouring without making additional incisions. The liposuction doesn't add much time or risk to the surgery when performed appropriately. About one-half to three-quarters of my patients choose to do liposuction with their gut tuck (more about this in the next chapter).

When you visit my office for an evaluation, I'll illustrate these procedures using a button-down shirt. The shirt button directly overlying the belly button marks the incision site for belly button release. The larger incision is where the shirt tucks into pants. I dissect up under the shirt toward the rib cage. Once that is complete, the tightening of the rectus plication into more of a v-shaped torso is performed. Next, I pull the shirt down, and any bunched-up excess is removed. The belly button is repositioned in a more youthful and vertical position, and the lower incision is closed, leaving you with a smoother, flatter, younger-looking gut.

From start to finish, a gut tuck takes anywhere from two and a half to four hours. If your belly overhang is small, the surgery can be even shorter. Liposuction to the love handles adds about thirty minutes to the procedure.

AFTER THE GUT TUCK SURGERY

A gut tuck is an outpatient procedure; only rarely would you have to spend the night in the hospital. I'd much rather send you home than subject you to the risk of a hospital-acquired infection and to the interruptions to your rest (such as a nurse waking you up in the middle of the night to ask how you're sleeping). You will be much happier at home in a familiar setting.

A gut tuck is a very safe procedure and generally goes very smoothly. If you're young and healthy, the risk of complications is low. We do, however, carefully monitor for blood clots in the veins of your calf muscle (deep vein thrombosis or DVT), where blood clots most commonly appear. While this likelihood is minimal (less than 1 percent, and most commonly occurring between five and fourteen days post-surgery), if it does happen, it can be very dangerous. The best way to prevent DVT is to use these muscles to circulate blood by walking. I insist that all my patients walk a short distance, with assistance, the night of the surgery, and a minimum of three times a day thereafter.

The recovery period after a gut tuck lasts about two weeks. The first night after the surgery is usually not too difficult, because you will still be enjoying the effects of the anesthesia and the numbing medications I use for the incision. Days two, three, and maybe even four will likely be the most uncomfortable. You can expect some pain, and you probably won't be very excited about getting out of bed much. You still *must* get up and walk, however, to prevent a blood clot. Pain medication can help quite a bit during this period. I typically send you home with these, along with muscle relaxants and anti-nausea medication, which can help prevent vomiting with sore gut muscles. If you are taking these medications, be very cautious and ask for help when you are getting up.

You can eat normally as soon as you feel like it. Most patients start off with bland food—crackers and ginger ale are recommended. Pain medications are notorious for causing constipation, so you may want to include salads and other vegetables for the fiber, or try some over-the-counter medications to help with this. On the flip side, you may find that you need to urinate more than usual for the first few days after surgery. That's a good thing—and will also get you out of bed regularly.

I allow my patients to shower after two days. We have found this goes a *long* way toward helping you feel human again, which speeds the recovery along.

As you recover, you will continuously be wearing a tight compression garment around your torso. For the best results, it should be worn 24-7 (except when showering) for the next six weeks.

Getting in and out of bed seems to be one of the biggest challenges during recovery, because of the soreness in your abdominal muscles. We'll teach you how to log roll onto your side and push up with your arms to get in and out of bed. It's the best way to avoid straining the muscles and to minimize the discomfort.

For the first few days, you will likely have some temporary drains in place to remove the expected fluid buildup and prevent pressure on your incisions. Whenever I move skin and fat to a new place (remember the "window shade"), it tends to rub against the other tissues and secrete fluid. This is absolutely normal and expected. We'll teach you how to easily manage these drains while at home.

During the postoperative healing period, it's important to note that swelling after surgery tends to go into the groin and potentially into the scrotum. There may be some swelling and bruising in these areas, but this is simply due to the collection of fluids and the influences of anatomy and gravity—not because the areas were operated on in any way. During this time, it may help to wear more supportive undergarments such as briefs or a jock strap until the swelling subsides.

Within a week of the surgery I will see you in my office for a postoperative visit and to remove the drains. Once the drains are out, you can gradually resume your normal activities. For the next three months, you should avoid straining the abdominal area—no heavy lifting, crunches, or core workouts. I normally release my patients to resume most activity and exercise (with the exceptions mentioned above) within two weeks of surgery. It's okay to resume having sex whenever you feel up to it; you may need to be creative in positioning to avoid strain and discomfort. As always, I recommend that you listen carefully to your body as to how intense your activities might be.

GUT TUCK: SCARRING AND HEALING

The scar from the gut tuck heals up quickly and becomes almost invisible within a couple of years. It will never go away completely, but it will definitely fade down to where it is very close to normal-colored skin, perhaps with just a slight discoloration. To minimize the scarring, we ask that, at the three-week point, you start lightly massaging the area with a silicone-based scar cream. Plain old Vaseline seems to work really well, too. The real key is to use something that lubricates the skin as you massage it—and to be gentle with the scarred area to avoid damaging it. I have seen allergic reactions to antibiotic ointments or vitamin E. When I see scars that have turned red, I always ask first, "What are you putting on it?"

Poor wound healing is another minor hazard. In almost every case, the wound heals quickly and cleanly. A preexisting health problem like diabetes can cause a patient to heal more slowly. In rare cases, the midline part of the incision, where the tension is greatest, can become infected, or the skin can break down and cause wound-healing complications. Sometimes we see poor scarring. For reasons we don't really understand, some people form keloids, a tough, thick scar that rises up above the skin. Sometimes the scar is asymmetric (or "catawampus," as they say in Tennessee). This usually happens if the abdominal flap is pulled down unevenly, too tight on one side or not tight enough on the other. We can sometimes see "dog ears," little overhangs or puckers in the skin near the far ends of the incision. These often go away within a few months. If necessary, we can easily do a little scar revision in the office under local anesthetic.

YOUR GUT TUCK OVER TIME

Almost everybody heals up quickly from a gut tuck, and the scar gradually fades away to near invisibility. In the long term, the major concern is weight fluctuation, which could stretch out the skin in the abdomen all over again and create more stretch marks (sometimes worse than before, as your skin is tighter from your surgery). However, if you keep your weight in the normal range and stay reasonably fit, the results should stand up well, with no major risk of drooping or stretching.

INNIE? OUTIE? JUST MAKE IT A "NORMAL" BELLY BUTTON

With the gut tuck surgery, we will reposition the belly button, but some men come in for issues related solely to their belly button. I had a massage therapist complain that every time he leaned over a patient and strained, he popped his belly button out. In reality, he was squeezing a piece of his intestines through the hole next to his belly button and feeling the bulge. We often think of this bulge as the hernia, but the opening or hole itself is technically the hernia.

Umbilical hernias can be genetically inherited or can be acquired through straining or vigorous exercise. Usually this is an isolated defect and can be dealt with in a fairly inconspicuous manner. Occasionally it can be part of a larger defect that might involve the assistance of a general surgeon. To correct an isolated umbilical hernia, typically a curved incision is made around the bully button. The defect or hole is then identified. The abdominal contents making up the bulge are reduced, placed back inside the abdominal cavity, and the hole is closed tightly with sutures to prevent recurrence. Occasionally, a synthetic mesh or screen is used to avoid extra tension and ensure longevity of the repair. The belly button is tacked back down to the rectus fascia, the strength layer, and the skin is sutured closed. The overlying scar is hidden within the confines of the belly button.

The surgery takes about an hour, often much less, and can be done on an outpatient or in-office setting. Recovery from the isolated umbilical hernia repair is quick, with the only restriction being to avoid heavy lifting or strenuous activity for six weeks to allow the repair to become as strong as possible.

LIPOSUCTION

You've been to the gym, you've watched what you eat, but you still have those stubborn love handles, or that extra layer of fat around your chest, abdomen, or even arms.

Don't blame yourself. Many times, those stubborn areas harbor excess fat that is unreachable by diet and exercise alone. Even though you can't tone those areas away, you don't have to put up with them. You can choose to get rid of them with liposuction.

With liposuction (also known as lipoplasty or liposculpture), I remove small amounts of subcutaneous fat in specific locations in order to smooth and shape your appearance. But I can't suck away all your excess weight. In fact, I ask my patients to be within 20 percent of their optimal weight before I perform the procedure—it's not weight loss surgery or a substitute for weight loss. And it's important that you get to that weight through healthy eating and exercise, not crash dieting.

I ASK MY PATIENTS TO BE WITHIN 20 PERCENT OF THEIR OPTIMAL WEIGHT BEFORE I PERFORM THE PROCEDURE—IT'S NOT WEIGHT LOSS SURGERY OR A SUBSTITUTE FOR WEIGHT LOSS.

WHAT IS LIPOSUCTION?

Liposuction is where we remove those love handles and reduce the abdominal fat that isn't removed with the gut tuck. If you don't need a gut tuck, liposuction can be done on its own to good effect. We often do this in other areas such as around the chin to create a more chiseled look. Liposuction can also reduce areas of fat around the upper chest.

Liposuction means, literally, fat removal by suction, performed using specialized techniques and protocol. Several types of liposuction techniques and equipment are in use today, with various names or acronyms that seem to improve their marketability, not necessarily the results. The current most popular types are laser, power assisted, and ultrasonic assisted. For larger areas and/or areas with the more stubborn fat, I often prefer to use ultrasonic-assisted liposuction in combination with the well-proven tumescent anesthesia method.

IS LIPOSUCTION RIGHT FOR YOU? QUESTIONS TO ASK YOURSELF

☐ Have you made a real effort to lose weight?

☐ Are you within 20 percent of your ideal body weight?

☐ Do you have type 2 diabetes? Are you a smoker? Both can limit your wound-healing ability.

☐ Are your love handles and other stubborn fat deposits really upsetting you?

☐ Do you have realistic expectations? Liposuction can only remove small amounts of fat in selected areas. It isn't weight loss surgery.

☐ Will you continue to eat well and exercise after the liposuction? Weight gain will undo the liposuction benefits.

☐ Have you had previous abdominal surgeries or radiation treatment that produced scar tissue that could complicate the procedure?

In general, liposuction is a very safe procedure that works well if you've been eating well and working out, and are back to or close to your ideal weight but still have lumpy areas that just won't go away. If you are planning to undergo a gut tuck and are considering lipo, it would be best to combine the two procedures as you're already under anesthesia and planning some recovery time. Liposuction won't add much to your discomfort or slow down your healing greatly. If you choose liposuction alone, the recovery time is somewhat shorter than for the gut tuck.

THE LIPOSUCTION PROCEDURE

Liposuction is performed with tumescent anesthesia with or without general anesthesia—many patients combine liposuction with their other procedures, so a general anesthetic is helpful here.

I begin the procedure by using a thin, straw-like stainless steel tube called a cannula to inject the tumescent anesthesia—a mixture of a local anesthetic, a blood constrictor, and normal saline solution (sterile salt water)— into the areas to be reduced. This makes the fat walls swell up and makes them easier and less painful to remove. If needed, I'll next use an ultrasonic tip on the cannula to help break down the fat. The high-frequency sound waves make the tissue near the tip vibrate very rapidly, which helps break down the connections between the fat cells and makes them easier to suck away. Next, I'll move the cannula carefully around in a fan shape within the area to be treated to make sure the fat is removed evenly. As I move the cannula with one hand, I'll be feeling the area with the other to make sure I don't leave any bumps, ridges, or depressions in the skin when I suction out the combined fluid and fat cells.

If you are also having a gut tuck, I can insert the cannula into part of the area to be treated from the tuck incision. That means fewer scars. If you do end up with liposuction scars because I couldn't reach everything through the original incisions, they are very small—just small puncture marks no wider than your fingertip. I can often hide the scars in an existing skin crease. They heal up very quickly, and because I have placed an anesthetic directly into the lipo area, you have very little pain for many hours afterward. If your liposuction is in addition to a gut tuck, it really won't add to your post-op pain much at all.

Liposuction is quick. One of the longer parts of the surgery is waiting for the tumescent anesthesia to take effect. When combining liposuction with other surgeries, we can inject the tumescent fluid and work elsewhere while it sets up. With a combination of skill and efficiency, liposuction typically adds no more than an hour or two to your surgical time.

AFTER LIPOSUCTION

After a brief stay in the recovery area, lipo-suction patients generally go home. You'll notice right away that the areas that had liposuction may look worse now than they did before the procedure. That's because they're swollen from all the fluid I injected and from the effects of the surgery. The swelling and bruising will go down, but it will take several weeks or even longer for you to see improvement; it might be up to three to six months before the final result can be appreciated.

You'll be sent home wearing a close-fitting surgical garment to help with the swelling. Other than that, the postoperative instruc-tions are pretty minimal. If you've also had a gut tuck, you'll follow the post-op instruc-tions for that. We definitely see the best results when you wear the garment nearly all the time for six weeks.

If you had liposuction alone, you won't have much pain, just some soreness that will go away in a few days. I'll prescribe a mild painkiller to help alleviate that. Most of my patients don't need anything strong and stop taking even the mild meds after just a few days.

Liposuction is a very safe procedure, but there is always a very small chance of infection. As always, having type 2 diabetes or being a smoker could slow healing. The biggest complication of this surgery is contour irregularities. If too much fat is suctioned out of one particular spot, it can leave a depression in that area. When looking at the area as a whole, it can look a little wavy, or show as "peaks and valleys" in your skin. In my experience, I have found that I can minimize or avoid this issue altogether by using my opposite hand as a guide while performing the surgery.

Simply because of injected fluids working their way out, you might ooze a bit from your incisions the first night or two home after the surgery. Your body will have to absorb that fluid or push it out through the small incision holes. This fluid will sometimes be blood tinged or a light reddish color; that doesn't mean you're bleeding. As you begin to increase activity, even more fluid may appear. You shouldn't be alarmed by this. It's perfectly normal.

You can take a shower on your second day home (and it'll feel good!). Most of my patients begin to return to their normal activities within just a few days. Almost all are back to their usual activity level within two weeks.

You will visit me in my office within a week after the surgery to make sure you're healing well, and again in a month or so for a quick checkup and review of your progress. I will see you again after three more months just to ensure all is healing well.

DON'T "EAT THROUGH" YOUR LIPOSUCTION

A strong word of caution: if you gain weight over time, you can still put fat back into the area we worked on or develop bulges in areas nearby. That is, even though we're removing fat cells, which don't repopulate in the body, the remaining fat cells can expand and get bigger. And the weight you gain won't go where it used to because we removed a greater number of cells from those areas.

In other words, just because you've had liposuction doesn't mean you have free license to eat fast food all day. You'll still gain weight. So, to keep the best results from your liposuction surgery, try to maintain your normal weight and avoid big weight gains and losses.

FURTHER POSSIBILITIES

Sometimes the fat I remove during the liposuction procedure can be processed and re-injected into your body to help fill out areas that are wrinkled or a little too flat, or to add more definition to a desired area. Fat is transferred commonly to the eyes, cheeks, face, buttocks, or hands. For wrinkles, a small amount can be used to fill these in. If you wish and it's appropriate, I can even transfer some of your own fat into your buttocks to help fill out the area.

I can also transfer fat into the backs of the hands. Because we naturally lose fat from this area as we grow older, this is a place where we can really show our age. Transferring fat can rejuvenate the hands, fill in wrinkles, and give them a more youthful appearance— the improvement is often dramatic. The procedure is simple and fairly painless. You can expect some swelling and stiffness in your hands for a couple of weeks, but after that, you'll be back to your normal activities. And the improvement is *permanent.*

CHAPTER 16

THE ASSLESS DAD

On returning from a consultation with a plastic surgeon, a forty-five-year-old woman was bragging to her husband about the doctor's evaluation.

"He said I have the breasts of a twenty-year-old, the stomach of a thirty-year-old, and the legs of a thirty-five-year-old," she told him.

"Well, what did he say about your fifty-year-old ass?" her husband retorted.

"Funny," she said thoughtfully, "he didn't say anything about you."

There's a never-ending supply of anecdotes about plastic surgeons and all the procedures we do, but the rear end tends to be the more common butt of jokes (pun intended). But in the end, the butt is an important area of plastic surgery focus. Some guys just want to keep their pants up—you can only put up with uncomfortably cinched belts around your waist for so long—while others desire more definition to this area.

We've seen a lot of guys for just this reason— they're looking for buttock augmentation because, as their coworkers may have pointed out on more than one occasion, "You could drop a plumb line from the back of your neck to your ankles and it wouldn't hit a thing."

Buttock augmentation doesn't mean you end up looking like one of the Kardashians; it's about giving you just enough backside so that you can keep your pants on and your ass doesn't just disappear down the back of your legs.

JUST DO SOME SQUATS, MAN

Sometimes, exercises like squats and clean-and-jerks can increase the gluteus maximus muscle bulk and shape a bit. Routine exercise of this area can improve its overall shape. If you're looking to put on size, most trainers recommend using higher weights with fewer repetitions. However, some men just cannot get any sort of bulk or projection or anything with exercise. Are they forced to remain the Assless Dad? I say *no*!

BUTTOCK AUGMENTATION PROCEDURE

Buttock augmentation is a pretty easy procedure. Usually it's a fat transfer, where we take some fat from the belly or thighs and put it in the desired location. We usually add some liposuction to the lower back to give the area a little more definition.

After removing the belly or thigh fat, we treat it in one of a number of different ways (centrifuging, straining, washing, rinsing with various agents, decanting ...the studies are, as of yet, inconclusive as to the best method) and then insert it into the buttocks through an incision about as wide as a pinky finger, one or two on each cheek.

From here the new fat can be worked in superficially or it can be injected deeper so that it intervenes with the muscle. There are different schools of thought on which procedure is more effective, but in my experience, both have had good results, and the technique we use is always customized for the individual.

BUTTOCK AUGMENTATION RECOVERY

Recovery from this procedure is about a six-week process, during which time you can't lay down on your back or you risk squishing the fat in the wrong directions. Because of this risk, we'll typically give you a compression garment to wear during recovery that looks similar to assless chaps: they have an opening at the butt where the fat was inserted and everything else is compressed.

During recovery, you'll need to lay on your side or your front while sleeping. Sitting is okay, but you can't do the old "executive in the swivel office chair" lean where you're tipped way back in your chair, as this puts pressure in the wrong areas. You can, however, sit straight up, as this position allows you to sit on the lower part of your rear, which is mostly bone and is below the area where the augmentation was done.

Like any fat transfer procedure, some of the fat that was moved will be reabsorbed. After a few months, we'll have an idea of what will stay around permanently. One thing to keep in mind with any fat transfer procedure is that the fat behaves like it is still from where it came. So, if you preferentially carried your fat in your gut, once this fat is moved to the buttocks, it will still expand like it did when it was in your gut. For some, this is an advantage, for others, not so much.

CHAPTER 17

WEDDING TACKLE

There are too many jokes to even start talking about it this chapter, so I'll leave it to you to fill in the blank [insert penis size joke here].

Once guys get over the jokes, however, they usually have a lot of questions, the biggest one being (pun intended), "Do you do male enhancement?"

The first guy who figures this one out is going to be a bazillionaire, but until he does, there really aren't a lot of options for extending your member except through urology mechanisms, and even those aren't incredibly effective. Penile prosthetics and pumps, for instance, are usually just used for the erection aspect, not to make you physically bigger.

FAT TRANSFER

The techniques used to increase the overall size of the male member have had lackluster results. For instance, there's the fat transfer procedure, but this usually ends up making you wider as opposed to increasing your length. And a lot of the time the results are unimpressive, leaving your penis with a soft, lumpy consistency that makes it look and feel like a hotdog in a bun. Even when you're erect, it'll have that soft, squishy consistency on the outside. This is the fat transferred to the outside of your original penis.

"LONG BUT LIMP"

Another procedure designed to lengthen your manhood involves cutting the suspensory ligament at the top aspect of the shaft near your pubic bone. The result is basically the same as what happened to Gene Simmons when he cut the frenulum on his tongue: it got longer, but only by about a centimeter or two. And because the tongue is the strongest muscle in the body, it could still move around, while the penis might lose that ability once the suspensory ligament is cut. In other words, you can get hard, but it's not going to jump to attention. Instead, it just tends to sit there like a sword in your pocket. Not ideal.

"SCROTOX" SWEAT REDUCTION

Back when I was still in residency, we took on a case with the urologists to address a nasty infection on a patient that required us to remove the majority of the skin from his scrotum and a little bit from his shaft. Because of the loose-skin nature of the scrotum, however, we were able to stretch the remaining skin upward, and we not only covered and tightened up his scrotum but also recreated the lost skin on the shaft of his penis. This resulted in a smoother-looking scrotum. The big joke after that procedure was that I was going to go into practice as the King of Scrotal Rejuvenation.

Even though I decided against keeping the title, we have done a number of procedures involving the scrotum, occasionally in order to reduce excessive sweating through the use of Botox injections. This side effect of Botox isn't brought up as often as its de-wrinkling capabilities, but the neurotoxins in Botox can do wonders for sweat reduction. When administering the Botox, we're careful not to "iron out" the scrotum too much, as that extra space serves as a body temperature regulator, allowing the testicles to drop away from the body when it's hot and pulling them in when it's cold.

In regards to the anti-wrinkling capabilities of Botox, it has been used as a cosmetic procedure down there as well. Botox injections can work to counteract the tightening forces of the smooth muscle of the scrotum, allowing the testicles to drop further in the relaxed skin. This makes the testicles appear "bigger" and "heavier," and thus gives the impression of enhanced masculinity.

Scrotox isn't an easy sell—guys have a hard enough time with the idea of getting Botox injections in their face, let alone their crotch—but if you're dealing with excessive sweat in that area, then it might be beneficial to learn more about this procedure in a private session with a board-certified plastic surgeon or urologist.

VASECTOMY AND VASECTOMY REVERSAL

The question often comes up of whether these procedures are part of the Daddy Do-Over. Many dads feel that once they are finished having children, they are "required" to undergo a vasectomy as a "rite of passage." Others have regretted this decision (especially those getting married for the second time). While each procedure is a very personal and individual decision that will affect not only the dad, but his family as well, neither is required for a Daddy Do-Over. I even hesitated to include the topics in this book. However, while a vasectomy and/or vasectomy reversal may be thought of as part of a Daddy Do-Over, this is typically handled by a urologist, not a plastic surgeon.

CHAPTER 18

YES, I HAVE REGRETS

TATTOOS

I have more comedic stories about tattoo regrets than I could ever remember. For instance, there was the one guy who had a pile of excrement tattooed on his belly with the word "Stanky" because his grandmother called him that as a child due to his smelly diapers, and another guy with a jailhouse tattoo of a woman riding a giant tongue on his arm.

A lot of us have regrets about our tattoos, especially as we age and the tattoos not only lose their significance, but also begin to warp and sag as our bodies change. But tattoo removal isn't as easy as just taking a laser and burning it off. Tattoos are made to go into the dermis, a deeper layer of skin immediately below the outer layer epidermis, which is why they're permanent. In order to get them out, you've basically got to take out the full thickness of the skin in the same way you'd remove a skin cancer or skin lesion. Tribal bands, for example, are some of the toughest to remove because they're usually etched in places where there's not a lot of extra skin to draw from, such as the shoulder, biceps, or wrist.

Laser treatments are certainly an option, but the process doesn't work like an eraser. Instead, the laser often just fades the ink until it has the dim appearance of a jailhouse tattoo. It lessens, but it doesn't get rid of the image entirely.

There are some different lasers coming out with better techniques that are designed to hit specific colors in the tattoo, basically blasting them open so that the ink breaks down into smaller particles that your body can absorb, but the technology is expensive and still being explored. However, when used with some of the more advanced pigments being used in tattoos these days—the ones that are capable of breaking into smaller particles—the removal results are improving.

A board-certified plastic surgeon can give you a good idea of what's possible with tattoo removal, depending on the location and age of your ink.

EAR GAUGES

I'll never forget this one guy who came in to have his earlobe repaired after trying to shove a frozen energy drink through his ear gauge hole. He got it in there, but the skin necrosed, cutting of the blood flow, and his ear lobe popped. He came in with that length of detached ear lobe just hanging in the breeze like a certain doofy cartoon character who is friends with a famous mouse. Before we began the procedure, he asked if he could keep the bit we were taking off. He'd apparently named it "Ricky" and wanted to keep it in a jar on his mantle.

We're all about patient satisfaction, so we were happy to oblige. As for the surgery, we ended up having to recreate his whole ear lobe.

It's surprising how many patients, men and women, we see for ear gauge repair. Many of them are surprised that the skin doesn't spring back after they take out the gauge, but just like any other part of the body, you can only stretch out the skin of the ear lobe so far before it won't retract—the elasticity of the skin won't take hold, and you have to get the lobe surgically repaired.

We see a lot of people who are going into the military needing this surgery, mainly because they can't serve with large ear gauge holes; they're considered a physical liability because they can get caught on something or someone can snag them.

EAR GAUGE REPAIR PROCEDURE

The repair procedure can range from simply splitting the skin down the middle and stitching it back into a normal position, or using a Z-plasty approach, where we inter-digitate the tissue and stitch it together in a zig-zag, similar to how you'd lace your fingers together. Or, in the most severe cases, as in the example of "Ricky" and his owner above, a total earlobe reconstruction needs to be performed.

TONGUE SPLIT

This trend is a hard one to repair, as it requires the tongue to stay completely immobile while it's healing, which is virtually impossible, as the tongue is in constant motion. The two halves of the tongue need to be lined up in the muscle layer and the skin over the muscle repaired. Any motion that occurs while the healing takes place could shear the two sides from each other, causing the tongue to heal improperly or not at all.

CHAPTER 19

FRINGE PROCEDURES

CALF, CHEST, AND ABDOMINAL IMPLANTS

These procedures are more often found in beach-type communities, and in my opinion they tend to look very unnatural as there's often not a lot of room to expand the skin in these areas.

Because of the lack of skin, getting these implants in is usually a sequential process. First, the skin has to be expanded so that the implant will fit. This is usually done with tissue expanders, which are essentially balloons placed under the skin for several weeks that are slowly inflated until the skin stretches and grows enough over the top of it that the implant can be inserted.

The people who do these types of things are often in some type of exhibition business, such as professional wrestling or the carnival. Many times, they think the rest of their body is perfect; they just need bigger _____, calves for example. My answer to this is to just hit the weight room and build it up; avoid the long procedure and unnatural results.

Abdominal implants are the same way. You can do some high definition liposuction sculpting around the abdomen, although the appearance of those muscles will alter over the years as the skin stretches and the abdominal muscles displace, but implants tend to look unnatural from the beginning. For one, they're incredibly hard to place inconspicuously and where they won't move. Again, this is an instance where I would recommend doing what you can at the gym and accepting your body and what it's able to accomplish.

HEIGHTENING PROCEDURES

This fringe procedure is one that seems to involve a lot of pain for very little gain. There are opportunities out there to get a little bit taller, but they're extremely invasive and result in very little height gain—maybe half an inch to an inch at most.

The procedure stems from an orthopedic specialty designed to repair shattered shins after traumatic accidents such as car wrecks. Essentially, two spoked wheels are placed around the patient's ankle and the top of the calf, and the spokes are attached directly to the bone. The two wheels are then driven apart, lengthening the distance between the two over time and forcing your body to create bone to fill in the space. It's not a quick procedure, either, and similar results can be achieved just by wearing shoe inserts or cowboy boots.

CHAPTER 20

BOTOX IN MEN: BROTOX, PROTOX, SCROTOX

S ince Botox has been so popular with men, even considered by many as the "gateway drug" into plastic surgery, and since many men only do Botox treatments and nothing else, I feel it deserves a chapter all its own. In this chapter, I gather together the highlights of discussions about Botox from earlier chapters in one convenient location—plus some additional information that hasn't come up previously.

Botox has gained wider acceptance among men as of this publication and is on par to reach popularity similar to that among the female population. Many factors have impacted the rise in Botox use among men, including the increased pressure in recent years to maintain a more attractive, youthful look in a highly competitive job market. It is a quick, easy procedure with zero downtime and typically fits in well with the busy male lifestyle. As the aging standard for men continues to increase, Botox is experiencing higher popularity. In fact, according to a study in the *Journal of Cosmetic Dermatology*, the number of American men getting injections has increased over 250 percent—just in the past ten years.[22]

Botox, Dysport, and Xeomin are all effective formulations of this toxin. For ease of use, I'll use the word "Botox," the name of the most

22   U. Wollina, and A. Goldman, "Minimally invasive esthetic procedures of the male breast," *Journal of Cosmetic Dermatology* 10, (2011): 150–155.

popular formulation, to mean any of these three drugs.

Botulinum toxin is a substance used to selectively paralyze muscles that form wrinkles. Some muscles have attachments directly to overlying skin and, when contracted, tend to pull skin inward. Done repeatedly, this leads to wrinkle formation. When this contractile force is removed for a time, these wrinkles naturally regress. Once the toxin wears off, the muscle function is regained at near full capacity. Over time, we can selectively atrophy these muscles so that their contractile forces are not as strong and less neurotoxin is needed to achieve the desired effect.

Initially, Botox was approved for a painfully spasmodic condition of the neck called cervical dystonia (or torticollis), which contracted the neck at such severe angles that many would actually permanently cut these muscles for relief. When Botox was injected, there was noticeable relief of the spastic pull of the muscles and the patient felt some relief. From there, the uses have expanded. Currently, Botox and its counterparts are FDA approved for treatment of cervical dystonia, upper limb spasticity, and temporary improvement in the appearance of wrinkles in the glabellar (between the eyes), crow's feet, and forehead areas.[23] Other uses have been performed safely and legally, and are considered "off-label" only because the FDA didn't initially approve its use for these conditions.

BOTOX FOR SWEAT AND MIGRAINE REDUCTION

Botox has been effectively proven to reduce sweating and migraines and is quickly gaining popularity for these uses. In fact, after the discovery of Botox use with spasticity in the neck, it was discovered that by

23   "Highlights of Prescribing Information," Allergan Pharmaceuticals, last revised October 2017, https://www.allergan.com/assets/pdf/botox_cosmetic_pi.pdf.

injecting the toxins into certain muscles around the neck, it caused the nerves to not activate as much, significantly reducing the occurrence of migraines.

The injections also help with hyperhidrosis, or excessive sweating. I had one patient come in who was suffering from excessively sweaty armpits and had undergone laser treatment to reduce it, but the process hadn't worked well. We decided to try out Botox injections on one armpit to see how it did, giving him about fifty units, and the results were great. He didn't have sweating issues for almost eight months. Now he comes in twice a year, just before spring and right after summer, and he's good for the year.

Sweaty feet, too, can benefit from Botox injections, as well as excessively sweaty hands, which can be a deterrent in the business world, where lots of handshaking takes place every day. And don't forget about the Scrotox option (we'll discuss that below). Overall, it's important to know that you don't have to put up with excessive sweatiness in any part of your body. All you have to do is ask.

BROTOX, PROTOX, SCROTOX, SADTOX ...

With men, there seems to be a need in the general population to put a name to its uses:

BROTOX

Although I am not a huge fan of this moniker, Brotox has become the popular term for Botox injection in men. When it comes to application, men tend to need a stronger dose than women, mainly because we have bigger muscles and stronger facial features. The dose lasts about three to six months, and the strength of the injection can range from partial to total paralysis. Personally, I tend to favor partial paralysis, as it allows for some movement; we still want to have to some animation when we talk.

Popular areas for toxin injections in men include the glabella area, which is the spot right between the eyebrows (where the classic "11" lines form), the forehead, and around the crow's feet area of the eyes. Some people will also get Botox injections for a gummy smile or for the lower aspects of the jaw.

PROTOX

Protox has become the fashionable trend of professional men receiving these quick injections during convenient times during their work day. Many lawyers will stop in on the way to court, docs will catch me on their way to the hospital or operating room, and the financial advisor will zip in between appointments or before heading to the golf course. Because it is such a quick and painless procedure, Protox has become widely popular.

SCROTOX

This one is a harder sell for many men. Scrotox is a term used for Botox injections into the scrotal area. Botox can do wonders for sweat reduction, and the scrotal area can be an embarrassing area for men who have excess sweating. When administering the Botox, we're careful not to "iron out" the scrotum too much, as that extra space serves as a body temperature regulator, allowing the testicles to drop away from the body when it's hot and pulling them in when it's cold.

Botox has been used as a cosmetic procedure down there as well. Botox injections can work to counteract the tightening forces of the smooth muscle of the scrotum, allowing the testicles to drop further in the relaxed skin. This makes the testicles appear "bigger" and "heavier," thus giving the impression of enhanced masculinity.

SADTOX

Sadtox is the term I use when we use Botox to treat depression. We have certain muscles that cause us to frown. If we can prevent these muscles from working well enough, we actually might just feel better. Dr. Eric Finzi and Dr. Norman Rosenthal published a study in 2014 that showed significant improvement in the moods of patients with major depressive disorder after a single treatment of a neurotoxin.[24] Even if we don't have major depressive disorders, I believe Botox can help us feel happier. I often will have my patients perform a corny exercise that I challenge you to do as well. If you force yourself to smile for five continuous seconds, you'll find that it is almost impossible not to have an elevated mood. So with Botox, we prevent the reverse of this silly exercise: we can't frown as strongly and we are, by

---

24   Eric Finzia, and Norman E. Rosenthal, "Treatment of depression with onabotulinumtoxinA: A randomized, double-blind, placebo controlled trial," *Journal of Psychiatric Research* 52, (2014): 1–6, http://www.botoxfordepression.com/wp-content/uploads/2014/03/Finzi-Rosenthal-Article-FINAL-copy.pdf.

default, forced to be less grumpy. Might be worth a try.

BOTOX PROCEDURE

Botox is administered with tiny injections and can leave a small welt of skin that dissipates within five minutes or so. With forehead injections, we'll often start at the top and correct some of the horizontal wrinkles of the forehead, then move down to the area between the eyes, being careful to add enough to reduce the wrinkle but not so much that it completely paralyzes the area.

Since men tend to need stronger doses of neurotoxin, we'll probably do between twenty-five and fifty units of Botox between the eyebrows and about sixteen to twenty units along the forehead, injecting the solution with incredibly fine needles similar in size to the kind diabetics use to prick their fingers four times a day. Despite this, some guys get a little antsy when we come at them with a needle. In those cases, we'll offer some numbing cream before doing the injections.

Botox injections tend to last about four months on average, and there's zero recovery time after a procedure. In fact, some clients will come in during their lunch break or before they go into work for the day. The effects take about a week to kick in, gradually setting in, until clients start to notice that they can't flex the injected muscles as strongly as they used to, or they can't furrow their brow as aggressively. When it starts to fade off, too, the effect is just as gradual.

PRECAUTIONS WITH NEUROTOXINS

There's a twofold precaution that people should be aware of when considering Botox: The first part is that if a neurotoxin is injected improperly and strikes an artery that feeds into the eye, it can cause permanent blindness. The second part of that precaution, then, is self-explanatory—don't allow anyone who isn't board certified to do a

Botox injection on you. Only board-certified plastic surgeons, dermatologists, oculoplastic surgeons, and facial plastic surgeons, or those who are overseen by them, should do this procedure, as they're the only ones who truly understand the deep anatomy of the skin. An aesthetician or physician's assistant may not have this knowledge, and certainly not some hair dresser or day spa employee. Neurotoxin injections are a medical procedure, not a spa treatment, so be certain you're seeing a professional when you have this procedure done.

CHAPTER 21

HEALTHY EATING TO MAINTAIN YOUR DADDY DO-OVER

E ating well and drinking lots of plain water will help your body recover well from any of the procedures you end up going with. There are a number of foods that are especially helpful for maintaining the results of your Daddy Do-Over.

Foods high in antioxidants will be very beneficial. They are easy to recognize, since most are quite colorful. Blueberries and pomegranates, for instance, contain antho-cyanin, which helps protect your skin from fine lines and dryness. They also provide lots of vitamin C, which you need to produce collagen and reduce wrinkles. In general, all colorful fruits and vegetables are high in antioxidants, which prevent the free radical damage that can be the precursor to fine lines and wrinkles that age your skin.

Orange vegetables, including sweet potatoes, carrots, and butternut squash, contain beta carotene, which your body converts to vitamin A and to retinol, which helps smooth the skin and protect it from sun damage. Spinach and kale are other great sources of beta carotene.

Dark chocolate—in moderation—is another great choice. It's full of antioxidants and fla-vonoids, which help with skin repair.

Walnuts, fish, avocados, flax seeds, tofu, soy milk, and edamame (soy beans) are all great sources of omega-3 fatty acids, which help provide smoother skin and healthier hair. The soy foods also contain isoflavones, which help reduce inflammation and can help stave off collagen breakdown to improve your skin tone and minimize wrinkles. Fish oil capsules are also a good source of omega-3s, but be cautious with these as they can thin the blood. If you are planning any sort of surgery, stop taking them at least two weeks in advance.

Green tea is an excellent source of antioxidants, especially the kind called catechins. These can help prevent skin cancer and may help stave off damage from sunburn. Green tea also tends to have a lot less caffeine than coffee.

By sticking to a regular exercise regimen and incorporating these foods into your diet in moderation, you should be able to maintain your health and the results of your Daddy Do-Over.

THE DADDY DO-OVER IN ACTION

I f you've learned anything from this book, I hope it's that plastic surgery isn't a "ladies only" deal. Guys want to feel good about themselves, too. We want to look good and we want to maintain that confidence that seemed to come so easily when we were in our twenties. And we can do that naturally, without looking like a wax museum figure. It's amazing how just a few touches here and there can restore so much of a guy's youthful vigor and vitality.

Take this one dad who came to see me not too long ago. He'd always been in good shape, but after getting married and having a couple of kids, he wasn't able to hit the gym as often as he used to and was holding down two jobs that were just adding to his stress load. He had always been concerned with his chest's appearance, but the natural results of aging were getting more apparent. He'd begun a new workout regimen six months prior but still had some stubborn areas that wouldn't go away.

With his shirt on, he seemed in fine shape, but when he took his shirt off you could see where his areas of concern were: his belly and chest had a little bit of pudge to it, and there were some love handles that didn't look like they were going anywhere soon. He was basically the ideal candidate for a Daddy Do-Over—he was a guy whom fatherhood had really taken ahold of. While he was doing what he could to stave off the effects, there were some things that he just needed help getting rid of, and I was happy to help.

I have guys from every walk of life asking me about the different plastic surgery options out there, but it often takes a lot for them to make that call—and just walking into the office can be a Herculean effort. That's the main reason I wanted to put this book together. I want guys to have a way of finding out about these procedures without having to ask uncomfortable questions or feel like they have to ask someone else for help.

This book is all about information, and if some of what you've learned in these pages makes sense to you and you'd like to see what's possible, I'm happy to set up a confidential consultation.

I can be contacted via my website, www.musiccityplasticsurgery.com or by calling my office at (615) 567-5716.